BERLITZ®

MOROCCO

1986/1987 Edition

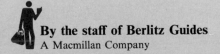

By the staff of Berlitz Guides
A Macmillan Company

15th Printing
1986/1987 Edition

How to use our guide

- All the practical information, hints and tips that you will need before and during the trip start on page 101, with a complete rundown of contents on page 104.

- For general background, see the sections Morocco and the Moroccans, p. 6, and A Brief History, p. 10.

- All the sights to see are listed between pages 20 and 79. Our own choice of sights most highly recommended is pinpointed by the Berlitz traveller symbol.

- Entertainment, nightlife and all other leisure activities are described between pages 80 and 91, while information on restaurants and cuisine is to be found on pages 92 to 100.

- Finally, there is an index at the back of the book, pp. 127–128.

Although we make every effort to ensure the accuracy of all the information in this book, changes occur incessantly. We cannot therefore take responsibility for facts, prices, addresses and circumstances in general that are constantly subject to alteration. Our guides are updated on a regular basis as we reprint, and we are always grateful to readers who let us know of any errors, changes or serious omissions they come across.

Text: Tom Brosnahan
Photography: Jean-Claude Vieillefond
Layout: Doris Haldemann
We wish to thank Shelagh Hyner and David Pulman for their help in the preparation of this guide. We're also grateful to Royal Air Maroc and the Office National Marocain du Tourisme for their valuable assistance.

Cartography: Falk-Verlag, Hamburg

Contents

Cover picture: Royal Palace, Fez

5

Morocco and the Moroccans

Morocco is a land where misty legend and modern life exist comfortably side by side. Its allure is special, and made up of many elements: the magnificence of a Moorish palace, the contentment of a humble cobbler working at his age-old trade, the scent of orange blossoms along a city street in spring. Diversity is the keyword, and in this land of fertile plains, snow-capped mountains, blazing deserts and flashing seas there are enough sights and stories to beguile for even more than a thousand and one nights. African, Arabian and European all at once, Morocco draws on many cultures. The Arabs call it *al-Maghrib*, the "land of the West", for to them it is the Atlantic bastion of Islam. Moroccans sometimes call their country the Sharifian Empire because their monarch is a descendant of Mohammed. To Africans, Morocco is a bridge of fertile land connecting the vast wastes of the Sahara with Europe beyond the narrow Straits of Gibraltar. Europeans find the country a perfect blend of the familiar and the exotic, with sightseeing in oriental bazaars by day and dancing in lively discotheques by night.

The three-part character of the land extends to the Moroccan peoples as well. The Caucasoid Berbers of mysterious origin have lived in North Africa longer than anyone knows, and they still keep their ancient traditions and lan-

guage. In the 7th century, Arab invasions brought to Morocco the seeds of the greatest civilization of medieval times, which flowered here and in *al-Anda-lous* (Spain). The Arabs have left their language, literature, and magnificent works of art for their descendants and the world to admire. And in the present century, European domination brought a medie-

Market-day is a weekly festival in Moroccan towns—a sempiternal magnet. Besides shopping, there's the latest gossip to catch up on.

val economy into the modern world, building roads, farms and factories.

Whatever your pleasure, Morocco has something to offer. Imagine swimming along shores once skirted by pirate ships, hiking among mountains where mythical Atlas held up the sky, or trekking through the desert to sun-baked fortresses *(kasbas)*. You can do all these things, but such pleasures are mere appetizers when compared to Morocco's main course, its four Imperial Cities. They are so called because each has at one time been the capital of a Moroccan empire or state.

Fez is the oldest and greatest of Morocco's Islamic cities, a place where modern industry and age-old crafts live together. The people of Fez take great pride in their Karaouine mosque, where one of Islam's oldest and most prestigious religious universities survives and prospers. By birthright, every man from Fez knows by heart the intricate spider's-web maze of the great *médina* (old town), a place so unfathomable to outsiders that an experienced guide is absolutely essential.

The second Imperial City, Marrakesh, is almost as old as Fez. Its role for close on a thousand years has been that of the country's southern stronghold,

lord of the High Atlas and the desert, where mountain people and Sahara nomads mingle easily with tourists and town dwellers. In Marrakesh, the traditional Berber way of life continues undisturbed.

Meknès, third Imperial City, is the Moroccan Versailles, built during the same era as Louis XIV's palace near Paris by a ruthless but sublimely visionary sultan who strove to give physical shape to his grandiose dreams. Today the ruins of tremendous palaces bear vivid testimony to a highpoint in Moroccan civilization.

Finally, Rabat is the capital city of today's Sharifian Empire. Where once pirates swaggered in the streets, now sleek limousines bear diplomats and ministers of state. Clean, cheerful, modern and of manageable size, Rabat holds tightly to its romantic traditions, and so for all its modernity the visitor cannot help but hear the faint echo of pirate cannons out of the city's past.

The magic of Morocco is sure to touch you, whether you visit for a week or a year, and you won't escape its spell.

Street scenes are like stage sets in the desert town of Tiznit where life hasn't changed for centuries.

8

A Brief History

Legend sets the beginnings of history in this north-western corner of Africa with the dawn of the gods, just about the time that Atlas and the other Titans who ruled the universe were overthrown during a heavenly revolution led by Zeus. The unlucky Titans were condemned to various sorts of exile and hard labour, and Atlas had as his task to hold the sky on his shoulders through all eternity. Many aeons passed, and the Titan was transmogrified into the mountain range which still bears his name.

So much for legend. The facts, as far as they can be ascertained, are these: in the Old Stone Age, the Sahara was a vast savanna roamed by animals that can now only survive in more southerly regions. But later the area progressively dried out, until some 5,000 years ago Morocco was virtually isolated by the sandy wastes. By the start of the historical era the Berbers (we know them by the name the Greeks and Arabs gave them) were already established here. No one knows where they came from, though theories link them with the Celts, Basques or even the Canaanites. They speak their own languages and

Elegant Moorish craftsmanship lives on: arcade built in 1960s.

keep their traditional customs even to our own day.

The Phoenicians, those great Mediterranean seamen and traders based on Tyre and Sidon, set up their first trading station in Morocco at Liks (Lixus) in about 1100 B.C. In the next millennium their descendants, the Carthaginians, founded further such posts, in-

10

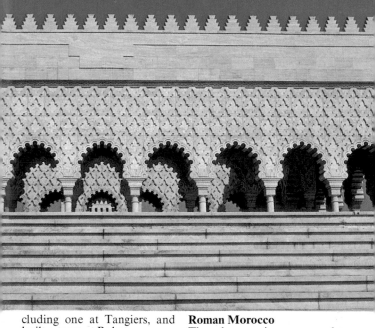

cluding one at Tangiers, and built a town at Rabat.

During the 4th and 3rd century B.C., small Berber kingdoms were being established in many parts of Morocco. Over a thousand years after these petty kingdoms flourished, the Berbers were to build mighty empires which ruled all of North Africa and parts of Spain. But in between these periods of Berber rule, Morocco was governed by outsiders: first the Romans, and later the Arabs.

Roman Morocco

Though marriages may be made in heaven, few young married couples come to be worshipped as god and goddess. But King Juba II and his young wife Cleopatra Selene were worshipped as gods in Roman Morocco. Juba was the son of a Berber king in Roman Africa. Brought up under the benign and watchful eye of Augustus Caesar himself, Juba received the best Roman education possible, and was later sent off as governor of the province of Mauretania (Roman Morocco and Algeria). As a wife, Caesar gave him Cleopatra Selene, daughter of Antony and Cleopatra, after the young king had ascended his throne in 25 B.C. He ruled for almost 50 years, encouraged commerce and industry, and made journeys to countries as far away as Arabia to gather material for the many books he wrote. Some of the finest bronze statues found at the Roman city of Volubilis are of Juba II, the well-loved king.

The Arab Empire
The wave of conquering armies which poured forth from Arabia in the 7th century is one of the most baffling phenomena in all history. Before the coming of the Prophet Mohammed, the Arabs were merely scattered tribes of Semites living in a hot and dusty land. To earn their daily dates and camel's milk, they traded by camel caravan or carried out raids on their neighbours. But in A.D. 610 a remarkable thing happened: Mohammed, a merchant in the city of Mecca, was chosen by God to be His Messenger.

In the early years of Islam (the word can be translated as "submission to the will of God"), believers were organized into a small, close-knit community headed by Mohammed himself. But as more and more people came to accept the faith, the community of Islam grew quickly; armies were formed and military operations begun. Within a century of Mohammed's death (in A.D. 632), Arab armies had conquered the whole Middle East (including Persia), North Africa and even parts of Spain and France.

Among the Arab generals were many dashing, impetuous men and great leaders, but none more so than Oqba Ibn Nafi, who led his raiding armies all the way to Tangiers by the early 680s, and only halted there because of the sea.

Oqba turned and headed south, leading his armies to the old Roman capital of Volubilis. From there he marched to what is now Marrakesh, and on to Agadir on the coast, and then even farther south to the borders of the desert. Here in southern Morocco he was surprised to find tribes of Berbers whose *men* wore cloths across their faces. He made no jokes, as they looked to be formidable opponents. These veiled men of the desert would one day rule all the lands he had so recently conquered.

Oqba died on his return march to Arabia, but in the next 30 years other dauntless commanders took his place. These Moors, as they became known,

Juba II, Roman Mauretania's god-king, voyaged extensively, then wrote his own "travel guides".

Moulay Idriss

As a monolithic state, the community of Islam didn't last long. It was too big, and contained too many different kinds of people—including many non-Moslems. Soon many regions were governed by local princes and potentates.

Nothing was better proof of

crossed the straits by boat and carried the banner of Islam into Spain and France. For the next six centuries, Islam was the predominant power in Spain.

nobility than being a descendant of the Prophet. One such was Idriss who arrived in 788 in Morocco, and quickly found his way into the hearts of the 13

Berber tribes at Volubilis. Moulay (literally "my master") ruled through Arab officers and kept an Arab bodyguard, but this did not bother the Berbers, who followed him willingly. His power and influence grew, partly because he had *baraka* (divine blessing). Too much success by Idriss alarmed the powerful Harun al-Rashid, caliph in Baghdad, and an assassin with a phial of poison was sent to insinuate himself into Idriss' group of followers. The poison did its work. The saint was buried near Volubilis, and the village which contains his tomb (and bears his name) is among the most sacred places for Moroccan Moslems.

A Berber wife bore Idriss II, who took over his father's task and continued building an impressive capital for the Idrissid empire at Fez, not far from Volubilis. His city grew in the area now occupied by the Karaouine mosque, and refugees from other great Islamic cities such as Kairouan in Tunisia and Cordova in Spain brought vitality to its cultural and spiritual life.

Idriss II died in 828, and his empire was divided between his sons. This weakened the state, but Fez remained the principal Islamic city in Morocco.

Nomad Conquerors: the Almoravids

The next Moroccan dynasty had its beginning in a very unlikely place, among those Berber tribes of the desert regions where the men rather than the women wore the veil (partly, no doubt, as protection against the rough weather in the desert). A young Moslem religious student named Abdullah Ibn Yasin came south from the region of Agadir to preach to the Berbers, and soon emerged as a spirited and vigorous leader. His teachings were based on the strictest discipline—missing prayers once meant a severe whipping. Even many Berbers accustomed to the hardships of life in the Sahara found Ibn Yasin's rules too harsh, and the leader and his band were soon pushed south across the desert. They built themselves a strong fortress-monastery on the sub-Saharan coast in Mauritania, and perfected their discipline. Soon they were ready for revenge, and a small army of these puritans swept northwards back into Morocco, wrecking drinking places, smashing musical instruments, and generally imposing their discipline. In 1056 they took Taroudannt, and in 1064 built a small fortress at Marrakesh.

For all their unpleasantness, the Almoravids (as they were known) began the great golden age of Moroccan art and culture. As they spread through Morocco, these unsophisticated desert nomads picked up many of the more civilized customs of the other Berbers and Arabs. They took off their veils and relaxed their rules somewhat. When they heard that the Moslem rulers of Spain were in trouble from Christian attacks, the Almoravids flooded into Spain under the outstanding generalship of Yusuf Ibn Tashfin in 1086. Yusuf was soon the most powerful Moslem monarch in all Spain and the Maghreb. His soldiers brought back many of the habits and appetites of the dissolute but highly cultured Moslems of Spain. Soon the richness of Moorish art and architecture was spreading throughout Morocco, especially to Yusuf's southern stronghold of Marrakesh. Though the ancient city of Fez gave up its primacy to Marrakesh, the Almoravids did see fit to build the dazzling and splendid Karaouine mosque in Fez.

Art and Empire under Almohads and Merinids

The powerful Yusuf Ibn Tashfin died in 1107. Some years later, a young Moroccan theological student travelled east to visit the prestigious Moslem colleges of the Arabian heartland. On his return, Mohammed Ibn Tumart was filled with fervour and began a conservative religious movement much like that of the early Almoravids. He was, to many people, impossible and unbearable. At one time he even disrupted a wedding procession, forced the bride from the saddle ("Women should walk!") and smashed all the merry-makers' musical instruments. Though Ibn Tumart received very many forceful admonitions to mind his own business, he also acquired a large following of zealots (and presumably music-haters). He and his followers, finding themselves less than well-received by the public at large, imitated the example of the Almoravids and withdrew to a fortress-monastery. Tumart's was at Tinmel, in the High Atlas between Marrakesh and Taroudannt. In this mountain retreat, he built up his strength.

Discipline and zeal again won the day, and the Almohad empire was formed by the 1140s. It was to last for over a century, and to bring Moroccan power and civilization to one of its highest points. Almohad **15**

Mighty mud-brick walls: once impregnable, now just picturesque.

rule extended from Morocco through Algeria and Tunisia to Libya, and deep into Spain. Andalusian Moorish culture won the hearts of the Almohads as it had those of the earlier Almoravids. Echoes of Spanish art can be found in the best Almohad buildings: the Koutoubia mosque and minaret in Marrakesh, and the Hassan mosque and Oudaïa *kasba* gate in Rabat. This flourish of Almohad culture also produced advances in the sciences, particularly in the Spanish dominions. The famous Moslem lawyer, physician and philosopher Ibn Rashid (Averroës) was but one of the shining lights in Almohad culture.

As the inevitable decline weakened the Almohads, their place at the centre of Moroccan life was taken by another Berber dynasty, the Merinids.

The hundred years of Merinid rule brought glory to Fez as Almohad rule had brought it to Marrakesh. To embellish their city, the Merinids constructed the "new" city of Fez, Fès el Jédid, and also undertook to build the two most exquisite *médersas* (religious colleges) in Old Fez,

velopments. Christian warships and pirates attacked the Moroccan coasts. By the early 1500s, Portugal held most of the important towns along the Atlantic coast of Morocco. Later in the century the Spaniards took over Sebta (Ceuta).

A family descended from the Prophet Mohammed, the Saadians, gained control of Morocco and tried to stave off the Christian attacks, but by the end of the Saadians, the great age of Moroccan independence and medieval grandeur was past. The early 1600s found the Saadians reposing peacefully in the glorious tombs they had built for themselves in Marrakesh.

the el Attarîn (1325) and the Bou Inania (1355). The tombs of the Merinid kings, now in ruins, still dominate Fez from a nearby hill. In Rabat, the massive Chella was their fortified cemetery. It was during Merinid rule in Spain that Granada's magnificent Alhambra was built.

European Incursions

In the years of Merinid decline, Christian Europe was entering the Renaissance. The power of the Christian princes grew as their wealth increased and as scientific progress was made. Soon the Moslem countries were falling behind in new de-

National Revival under the Alaouites

New national leadership emerged with the Alaouites, another family of Sharifians (descendants of Mohammed). By 1672 the Alaouites had control of Marrakesh, and the greatest early Alaouite sultan, Moulay Ismaïl (reigned 1672–1727), had come to power. Moulay Ismaïl was a man of powerful appetites (it is said he fathered over 1,000 children) with a thirst for glory. Forsaking the Moroccan imperial cities of Marrakesh and Fez, he built his own imperial Meknès. **17**

Everything about the city and its imperial palace was monumental.

Succeeding Alaouite monarchs could not keep up Moulay Ismaïl's standards of vigour and vision, and Morocco suffered several decades of anarchy and privation. Other capable Alaouite monarchs came to the throne, but by that time Christian Europe was so far ahead of the Moslem world in science and economy that domination by Europe was inevitable.

Franco-Spanish Protectorate
Resourceful Alaouite rulers played off one European power against another throughout the 19th century, but the odds against them gradually increased. Not only were French and Spanish interests in the country growing, but Germany now began to use Morocco as a pawn in its colonial designs.

In 1912, the entire country came under a European "protectorate". France, under the far-sighted and able administration of Maréchal Lyautey, now governed the larger part of the country, the centre and the south. Spain controlled the northernmost portion except for Tangiers, which became a special international zone.

The Protectorate brought the many benefits of European science, technology and culture to Moroccan life: roads and public utilities were built, agriculture and mining were encouraged. But these were turbulent years, and for young Moroccans growing up in the 1920s progress was worthless without independence. The crown prince of the Alaouite dynasty, who in 1927 at the age of 17 became sultan as Mohammed V, sympathized in silence.

Independence
In World War II France was split, and Moroccans who wanted freedom came out in the open to form the Istiqlal (Independence) Party. The sultan was on their side, but he had to tread carefully as the Protectorate powers might otherwise take action against him. After the World War, repression worsened, and finally Mohammed V and his family were deposed and exiled by the French. The sufferings and privations which the sultan endured for his people and his country made Mohammed V a symbol of courage and resistance to foreign rule. By 1955 the French were forced to recall the royal hero from house arrest abroad. He was hailed as the saviour of his country, and

Symbol of Morocco today. Casablanca takes pride in modernity.

saw his efforts rewarded by a treaty ending foreign occupation. By 1956, Morocco was again unified under the independent rule of an Alaouite.

Mohammed V had just embarked upon his ambitious plans for progress and development when he died in 1961, after a minor operation. The nation was shocked and dismayed at the untimely passing of the greatest Alaouite sovereign since Moulay Ismaïl. The beloved Mohammed V retains a very special place in the hearts of 17 million Moroccans. The crown prince ascended the throne as Hassan II, and continues to forge a more prosperous future for his country. With Spain about to withdraw from the Spanish Sahara, the king organized a Peace March *(Marche Verte)*. On November 6th, 1975 some 350,000 volunteers walked over the frontier between the two countries and reclaimed the former colonial territory, amidst popular fervour. The tripartite agreement between Morocco, Spain, and Mauritania was signed in Madrid in April 1976 and fixed the new frontiers officially. **19**

Where to Go

Of the many sights to be seen in this fascinating and beautiful country, Morocco's four Imperial Cities must be at the top of any list. It's here that the splendour and magnificence of past Moroccan empires is concentrated and the breath-taking artistry of Moorish craftsmen reached a highpoint. Strolling through the maze of the *médina,* gazing at monuments of Islamic architecture and retracing the steps of medieval Moslem kings are among the highlights of a visit to Morocco. And for a change of scene, try a trek into the Sahara, or a few days' sunning on a smooth, sandy beach.

Rabat

The first city of modern Morocco was the last of the *makhzen,* or Imperial Cities. A town called Sala had been here on the Bou Regreg estuary since the 3rd century B.C., but in the 10th century A.D. a *ribat* (fortified monastery) arose on a bluff at the western extremity of the estuary's south bank. The Imperial City grew from this humble start.

Rabat was an important town under the Almohads, who called it Ribat el Fath (Ribat of Victory). Walls were raised, the Oudaïa *kasba* provided for defence, and the Hassan tower was the beginning of a grand mosque.

The Protectorate set up its Residency-General in Rabat in 1912 with Maréchal Lyautey, and when Morocco regained its independence, the city became the administrative capital of the kingdom.

Moroccan Medley

Here, in a nutshell, are the most common Moroccan words you're likely to meet:

aïd	holy day
aïn	spring
bâb	gate
baraka	divine blessing
borj	fort
djébel	mountain
fondouk	warehouse, caravanserai
jamaa	mosque
jellaba	long-sleeved tunic
kasba	fortified part of *médina*
ksar (pl. ksour)	fortified village
médersa	religious school
médina	old town
mellah	Jewish quarters
moulay	master
moussem	pilgrimage, followed by festivities
oued	river
souk	market (streets)

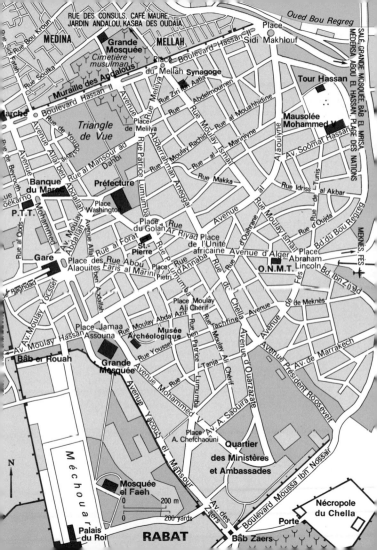

Modern Rabat

As the capital of a modern state, Rabat has many attractive public buildings and tree-lined boulevards, and is characterized by an easy-going, pleasant atmosphere. **Avenue Mohammed V,** main artery of the modern city, cuts a wide and sunny swath through the town, past government buildings, the railway station, the main post office and banks; pedestrians escape to the shady, shop-lined arcades and sleepy cafés along either side, leaving the roadway to the bustle and roar of motor traffic. Avenue Mohammed V is a place to stroll and browse, or to sip mint tea and plan your next activities.

No visit to the Moroccan capital is complete without a visit to the **mausoleum of Mohammed V,** erected by the nation to his memory.

A guard of honour of resplendent king's lancers watches over the tomb, and you will pass between a pair of these romantic warriors, mounted on their gorgeous steeds and sitting in the traditional high-backed Moroccan saddles, as you enter the complex. Though built during the 1960s, the tomb and other structures are the epitome of traditional Moroccan artistic opulence. The mausoleum proper, the adjoining memorial mosque and the separate pavilion all make use of bright brasswork, cool marble, various ornamental stones and polychrome tiles. In the mausoleum, the onyx sarcophagus rests at ground level, and visitors view it from a mezzanine above. A tremendous brass lamp swings slowly over the sarcophagus, suspended from a ceiling glowing darkly with rich gold ornamentation. Dashing guards with billowing capes and Berber rifles watch to see that propriety is observed both inside the mausoleum and on the terrace outside.

A constant stream of visitors, foreign and local, comes throughout the day to admire the artistry of the mausoleum, to pay homage to the country's former spiritual leader and father of its independence, or just to enjoy the sun-drenched courtyard.

In the museum and library adjacent to the tomb, memorabilia of the late monarch are on display.

The site chosen for the tomb of Mohammed V was next

Moorish architects of the Hassan tower worked tawny stone into a lacework still unsurpassed today.

to the ruins of the Hassan mosque, built by an Almohad sultan at the end of the 12th century. The sultan died before the mosque was completed, Koutoubia minaret in Marrakesh (and the Giralda tower in Seville, Spain). The decoration on the panels higher up seems almost to resemble

Oudaïa kasba *on the Bou Regreg: cannon peek coyly through its walls.*

and the main structure fell victim to the elements. The minaret, called the **Hassan Tower**, though also unfinished, has held up better and remains as a fine tribute to Almohad achievement, along with the stylized, ascending layers of clouds—an appropriately lofty and uplifting motif. The site, high on the banks of the Bou Regreg, is a superb one, and the view from the tower is equally impressive.

The Médina

The old town of Rabat is one of the more sedate ones, less "exotic" than the *médinas* of other cities described in this book. Though a good number of foreign tourists stroll through its streets and poke around in its shops each year, most customers are regulars, either Moroccan or from the diplomatic corps. Few little boys will approach you to offer their services as guides, few shopkeepers will harangue you passionately about the excellent quality and risibly low prices of their wares.

Travel north along Avenue Mohammed V, and go through the 17th-century **Andalusian wall** (*Muraille des Andalous*), pass the tidy market (*marché municipal*) on the left and then turn right into **Rue Souïka.** Though some shops along this street carry leather and copper items favoured by tourists, most are strictly for regular clients. Here you'll find what seems to be the world's largest assortment of transistor gadgetry, compressed into the smallest shops, the heftiest sheep's and beef trotters, and enough pairs of shoes to provide for an army of customers. After a few minutes' walking, the road enters the shaded **Souk es Sebat,** where you'll discover that modern department stores have nothing over Moroccan markets. In what store could you buy such an assortment of things: an exquisite gold ring, or a brace of sheep's heads, or a kilo of dried chick-peas (roasted or unroasted), or a new pair of comfortable yellow leather *babouches*—just the thing for slipping on and off easily when you go to the mosque for prayers?

Continue to the end of the Souk es Sebat and enter the bright sunlight again, turning left into **Rue des Consuls,** the *médina*'s most fascinating street for the tourist. Here are shops selling jewellery, carpets and antiques. Many have *caftans* and *jellabas*, and the shop-owners are often familiar with the clothing sizes and requirements of foreign customers. The street has a pleasant local atmosphere, with its many shopkeepers sitting contentedly before their wares, waiting to be of service and watching the parade in the carefully swept street.

At the end of Rue des Consuls is the massive and daunting **Oudaïa kasba** (*kasba des Oudaïa*), its walls laced with loopholes, its cannon still at the ready. The impressive, monumental **gate** to the 12th-century *kasba* is one of the Almohads' loftiest architectural achievements. Graceful for all its tremendous bulk, the horseshoe arches share the façade with long Arabic inscriptions in *kufic* script*. There are many nautical motifs, appropriate for this bastion of the Bou Regreg and the Atlantic: stylized seashells are everywhere, and at the pediments of the small ornamental pillars you can see the prows of boats. Stand back to gain the full effect of the five arched doorways which make up the gate.

The *kasba* is on the site of the *ribat* (fortified monastery) which gave the Moroccan capital its name. This is obviously the best spot from which to defend the city; in the 18th century the sultan Moulay Ismaïl transferred a tribe of fierce Oudaïa Arabs into the *kasba* for just that purpose.

Today the *kasba* is a residential quarter with iron-studded house doors in picturesque doorways. At the far end of **Rue Jamaa,** the main street, is an open area on the promontory overlooking the fortifications, the mouth of the Bou Regreg and Rabat's "sister city", Salé.

---

* There are two common kinds of Arabic script: *cursive,* elegant and free-flowing, and *kufic,* more angular and often with complicated, knotty designs on the uprights.

From here you can take a short flight of steps which leads down to a small restaurant and café overlooking the ocean. As you descend further, you can survey the Moslem cemetery, the jetty and lighthouse, and the Atlantic surf.

Another vantage point at the end of rue Lâalami offers a view upriver, over the crumbling fortress walls overgrown with moss and wild flowers, to the modern city. The Oudaïa *kasba* fulfills anyone's romantic vision of what a *kasba* should be.

For a restful break, descend along rue Bazzo to a pretty Moorish café, **Café Maure,** where tables are shaded by latticework and by the huge leaves of an ancient fig tree.

A door from the café leads directly into the *kasba*'s delightful **Andalusian Gardens** *(jardin andalou),* planted with everything from roses to bananas and "defended" by brass cannon with inscriptions that show they are either of 19th-century English or Spanish manufacture.

Leaving the garden by the ascending stairway brings you to Rabat's **Musée des Oudaïa,** the city's traditional arts museum.

The museum's courtyard is

that of a noble house built in the 1690s and recently restored. The collection includes blue and polychrome pottery, some very fine woodwork and much unusual gold and silver jewellery.

If time allows, pay a visit to the **Musée National de l'Artisanat** (6, Tarik el Marsa), a display of old furniture, rugs and ceramics. The crafts cooperative opposite *(Ensemble Artisanal)* sells the best modern work.

The Chella

The Roman town of Sala was on a site now outside the walls of Rabat. After the decline of Rome and of Sala, the Merinid sultans used the area as a cemetery and, in the 14th century, built a strong wall around it. Today the fortress is called the **Chella,** and besides saints' tombs and Roman ruins, it encloses a park which has a magical attraction for children. Enter through the imposing and ornate gateway, and descend the long path through gardens of plants familiar and exotic to a little grove of bamboo and banana plants. Here a cluster of seven ancient shops has been filled with water and is now a pretty pool. Slithery eels glide noiselessly in and out of the sunken doorways, children toss

Pirates of Salé

In the 17th and 18th centuries, the pirates of Barbary were a fearsome challenge to Christian supremacy of the seas. The fast and well-fitted Moslem privateers set out from points all along the Barbary Coast (the littoral of Tunisia, Algeria and Morocco). But the most celebrated corsairs in Atlantic waters were based in Rabat and Salé. These "Salley Rovers" as their English enemies called them, not only attacked Christian ships but also coastal towns in Spain, France and England. On at least one occasion Moroccan corsairs were seen operating in the waters off Newfoundland. Their last raid was in 1829.

coins in and hope for wishes to come true.

Not far from the pool a ruined mosque is now roofless, and gigantic trees grow where the faithful once prayed. Traces of tilework on the arches, doorways and especially on the minaret testify to former magnificence. Doorways on either side of the *mihrab* (prayer niche) lead to a pretty garden and a tomb decorated with arabesques.

Below the mosque is a **courtyard** with pools and fine decoration, and in the rooms nearby are vestiges of an extensive and

Luxurious vegetation amid saints' tombs, Roman ruins, enhance the haven of peace that is the Chella.

complicated plumbing system of terra cotta pipes. These were the public lavatories and baths, so important to a religion which requires ablutions before the five daily prayers.

The Roman ruins, up the hillside from the garden, are still in the process of excavation and are closed off, but a general view can give an idea of what ancient Sala was like.

Archaeological Museum

King Juba II would enjoy the congenial museum located in the new town that houses Rabat's collection of antiquities. An aerial photograph of Volubilis (the former Roman city 26 kilometres from Meknès) is a help to anyone in understanding the size and importance of that city. Exhibits are not limited to things Roman, however, for the collections cover all periods of Moroccan history from the Stone Age to the Alaouite dynasty. Keeping a **bust of King Juba** company in the fine (if sparsely furnished) Bronzes Room is a pretty statuette of *Ephèbe Couronné*.

Salé

Rabat's sister city at the mouth of the river Bou Regreg was founded in the 11th century. It flourished as a trading city in medieval times and had an active life of its own, but today the once-proud city is actually a suburb of Rabat. Salé remembers her past glories by preserv-

ing several impressive mosques, religious schools, and her own strong old walls.

Taking the road down to the Bou Regreg from the Hassan tower, you cross the river and come to the Bâb el Mrisa, the first gate through the Salé city walls. Enter the gate and wander through the *mellah*, or old Jewish quarter, to the centre of the town. Chances are you won't pass one tourist shop. Only the local people crowd to these markets, busy and colourful, fragrant with bundles of fresh mint for tea and crates of fruit and vegetables.

The Rue de la Grande Mosquée terminates at Salé's **Grand** **29**

Mosque, with its tall and imposing stone doorway at the top of a flight of steps. Though you won't be allowed to enter unless you're a Moslem*, you can visit the former religious college, the **Abou el Hassan médersa,** entered by the smaller door to the left. Knock on the door to bring the *gardien* or janitor, who guides tourists through the deserted building. Everything up to a height of about six feet is covered in tiles, and above the tiles are the traditional carved cedar and intricate **plasterwork**—among the finest and laciest in all Morocco. Little birds, who make their nests in the artfully carved wood eaves, dive-bomb visitors just for fun. Beat the birds by taking the stairs up to the roof.

On the way to the roof are two levels filled with tiny rooms for the theological students who came to the college. At the top of the stairs is your opportunity to peek into the courtyard of the mosque next door. From here, the **panorama** of Rabat, Salé and the river is incomparable, and all of the capital's landmarks are easy to locate.

---

* Throughout Morocco, entry to all mosques and other religious sites is strictly forbidden to non-Moslems.

Excursion from Rabat

Casablanca

Ever since the Portuguese took over this town on the Atlantic coast in the 15th century and renamed it Casa Branca (meaning "white house" in Portuguese), the main commercial port of Morocco has been the most European of the kingdom's cities. In the present century, under the Protectorate, it grew to become both the largest Moroccan city and also the centre of commerce and industry, known by the Spanish name it now bears (in Arabic, however, it's called *Dar Beïda*). It is a modern city in all respects, and even had there been impressive ruins from earlier times (which there weren't), doubtless they would have been quickly covered by the city's incredibly fast growth. Nearing a population of two million, it lies a mere 92 kilometres from the more sedate capital of Rabat.

Place Mohammed V is the cradle of modern Casablanca. At the turn of the century there was nothing but wasteland here. Now it and the surrounding area is a meeting-place of the city's major thoroughfares, alive with shops, cinemas,

NORTH-WEST MOROCCO

0 20 40 km
0 10 20 miles

ATLANTIC OCEAN

ALGECIRAS, GIBRALTAR, SÈTE, MARSEILLE

ALGECIRAS
Ceuta (Sebta)
Restinga
Smir
M'diq
Cabo Negro

MEDITERRANEAN

Ksar es
Seghir
TANGER
Cap Spartel
Grottes
d'Hercule
El Borj
Melloussa
Regaia
Oued Hachef
El Fendek
Souk el
Had el
Gharbia
Asilah
Souk Khemis
du Sahel
Lixus
Larache
Tleta
Rissana
Barga
Moulay
Bousselham
Lallo
Rhano
Sidi Mohammed
el Ahmèr
Souk Tleta
du Rharb
Benmansour
Mehdiya
Plage
Plage des
Nations
SALÉ
RABAT
PAYS ZEMMOUR
Sidi Yaliya
les Zaër
Âîn el Aouda
Had
Brachoua
Col de Kaour
Rommani
Gorges
PAYS ZAËR ZAÏANE
OUED ZEM

Souk Sebt
el Kdim
Dar Ben Karriche
El Bahri
El Manzla
912
Souk el
Arba Ayacha
Zaâroura
Souk el Arba
des Beni Hassan
1928
Derdara
Draa el Asef
Brikcha
273
Ouezzane
307
Col de Rmell
609
Djebel
Bou Hellal
Souk el Arba
du Rharb
Mechra
Bel Ksiri
Hau Huort
KÉNITRA
FORÊT DE LA MAMORA
Âîn Johra
Oued Sebou
Allal
Tazi
Morhrane
Dar Gueddari
Sidi Yahya
du Rharb
Sidi
Slimane
Msâada
Boumaïr
Dj. Tselfat
Sidi Kacem
406
Col du Zeggota
Dar
Bel Amri
Âîn ej Jemâa
Volubilis
1116
Moulay
Idriss
Moulay
Yacoub
Nzala Saraji
Karia Ba Mohammed
Pont du
Sebou
Jouaber
Dj. Zalagh
902
FÈS
Sidi
Âïn el Orma
Khemisset
Sidi Allal Bahraoui
Âit Yazem
Oued Tanerest
Tiflèt
Moulay Idriss
Arhbal
Mâaziz
Sebt des
Aît Ikkou
Boukchmir
Chebika
Source Karraba
El Harcha
Oulmès
Tiddas
400
Oued Berh
Oued Grou
El Haj
Kaddour
Boufekrane
Agouraï
1473
Ito
KHENIFRA
MIDELT
MEKNÈS
Dj. Zerhoun
Oued
Jaïda
El Hajeb
Barrage
d'El Kansera
Oued el Kell
MIDELT
Douyèt
Sidi
Ras el Ma
Harazem
PLAINE DU SAÏS
Âïn Cheggag
Bhalil
Sefrou
Immouzzèr
du Kandar
Ifrane
Azrou

TÉTOUAN
Taïfor
Bou Hamed
Ichtal
Chéchaouen
Bâb Taza
Mokrissèt
Zoumi
1595
Lalla Outka
Rafsaï
Ouirtzarh
Fès
el Bali
835
Mjâara
681
Dj. Amergou
Dj. Messaoud

BOUHACHEM
PAYS RHOMARA
Oued Laou
AL HOCEIMA, MELILLA
RIF
Oued Aoudou
Oued Aoula
PAYS DJEBALA
Dj. Kelti
1681
838
Dj. Haouz
Oued Makhazen
Oued Loukos
TAZA

cafés, travel agencies and crowds.

Nearby **Place des Nations-Unies,** with its substantial public buildings, is a major centre. The law courts, Préfecture, post office and tourist office, all conceived on a suitably grand scale, leave no doubt as to the official vocation of this part of town.

Meknès

In the late 17th century, Louis XIV of France was establishing a court of unprecedented splendour. At the same time, the second sultan of the Ala-ouite dynasty chose Meknès as his capital and set about building a city to rival Paris, a palace to rival Versailles. Moulay Is-maïl (reigned 1672–1727) went to work with his own hands and with those of every available slave, servant, captive Christian and local tribesman to shape his imperial town. Though much of his astonishing accomplishment is now in ruins, it is still a breathtaking sight to behold.

Blue jeans and caftan with veil symbolize the ancient and modern currents in Moroccan lifestyle.

Meknès had been a centre of some importance since the 12th century, but it was Moulay Ismaïl who put it on the map. His city, like his dreams, began to fade after his death, but the 20th century has brought rejuvenation. Today Meknès is a prosperous and active city, or rather two cities: the old Imperial City and *médina* on the west side of the Oued Boufekrane valley, and the modern town on the slopes of the eastern riverbank.

Imperial City

Though you will probably arrive in the new town, you should start your sightseeing with Moulay Ismaïl's Imperial City *(La Ville Impériale)*, and then continue along with a visit to the Meknès *médina*.

From the new town, cross the valley of the Oued Boufekrane and mount the hill to Place el Hédim, in the heart of the old city.

Dominating the southern end of the square is the lofty

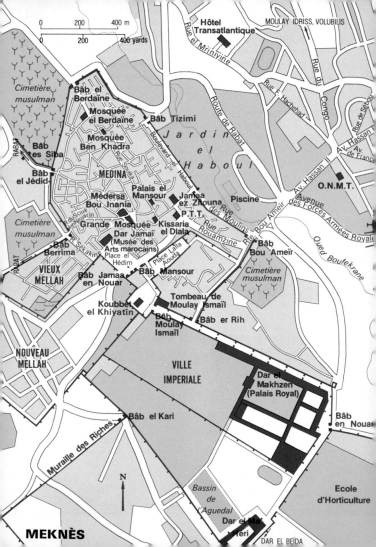

Bâb Mansour, an immense monumental gateway which at once takes you in spirit back to the Meknès of Moulay Ismaïl. The *bâb* (gate) is not one but actually several horseshoe-shaped doorways ornamented with clusters of marble pillars. The intricate, lacy patterns in relief and the rich, coloured tile panels echo the wealth and splendour of old Meknès and its imperial court.

The **Bâb Jamaa en Nouar,** to the right of the Bâb Mansour, is a smaller gate in a similar style—smaller, but still very grand.

The old imperial palace and town are so extensive that it's impractical to tour them on foot. If you don't take a tour by bus or private car, hire a taxi to take you around and show you all the sights.

Enter the Bâb Mansour, and you're on the great expanse of **Place Lalla Aouda,** which used to be just outside Moulay Ismaïl's tremendous palace. It was once, no doubt, the scene of many glittering parades and ceremonies (and perhaps a few beheadings?). A few government buildings now face the square.

Continue straight on from the Bâb Mansour and through a second gate, the Bâb el Filala, to another square. Where big sacks of sheeps' wool are emptied and the contents spread out for sorting and drying, ambassadors to Moulay Ismaïl's court once rode. The **Koubbet el Khiyatîn,** off to your right in the corner of the square, is where the great sultan received them with a maximum of pomp and ceremony. Underneath the pavilion are great cellars, perhaps for the rich presents which ambassadors of that day were supposed to bring to gain favour (legend also has it that these underground rooms served as dungeons for Christian prisoners).

On the opposite side of the square, a gate leads to the entrance of **Moulay Ismaïl's tomb.** The doorway to the tomb enclosure is magnificent, and like the rest of the tomb complex was renovated during the reign of Mohammed V. Once through the door, you pass through a succession of lofty chambers with fountains, where the sounds of footsteps echo off the yellow walls and tilework. At the threshold of the memorial mosque are grass mats, a signal to leave your shoes and proceed in stockinged feet. The tomb is a sacred place of prayer and pilgrimage, and non-Moslems are allowed to enter the little courtyard and to look into—but not to enter—

the sanctuary of the mosque proper. High up near the tiny courtyard's glass-covered roof is fine filigree plasterwork, with the unusual touch of bright painted highlights. The fine wooden doors, all done in intricate coloured designs, while not old are nevertheless good examples of this artistry. In the memorial mosque, the tomb lies below great, wide horseshoe arches which are somehow soothing; they give a sense of security, calm, strength and, above all, endurance.

Leaving the tomb again, turn left and pass through the **Bâb er Rih** (Gate of the Winds). No mere romantic name, the gate stands on two mammoth walls forming a corridor half a mile long: the perfect "wind tunnel". On the other side of the wall to the right is the royal palace (not open to visitors), where the monarch stays on visits to Meknès. At a corner in the corridor is a sturdy fortification called the Borj (or Dar) el Ma (Water Bastion). A little further along stands the capacious, partly ruined **granary** *(héri)* dating from the 17th century. Go up to the roof and its garden for a fine **view** of the city and of the huge Aguedal pool used for the irrigation of the vast gardens within the walls of the Imperial City. The palace

golf course occupies the site of the Garden of the Sultans. The area is open to the public, except when members of the royal family are in residence.

Attached to the granary are the remains of Moulay Ismaïl's tremendous **stables** *(haras),* which housed 12,000 steeds.

The horticultural school near the granary has beautiful experimental **gardens** open to visitors, which provide many shady, fragrant spots to rest.

A short distance from the granary stands the **Dar el Beïda,** a thick-walled fortress of vaguely Eastern European aspect. Built as a sultan's palace in the late 18th century, it now serves as a military officers' training school.

The Médina

A walk through the *médina* of Meknès provides enough fascination to fill a morning or afternoon. At the western end of Place el Hédim is an entrance gate to the *médina*, and right beside it is the door of the **Dar Jamaï,** private palace of a minister of state a century ago. Luckily for the visitor, the palace is now the regional

Courtyard of Bou Inania médersa exhibits delightful craftsmanship.

museum, officially called the **Musée des Arts marocains.** See the collections of masterpieces carved from wood, embroidered in silk and worked in metal; but don't neglect a close look at the palace itself. Bearing in mind that this fanciful architecture and arabesque decoration were not for the sultan but only for one of his ministers, imagine what splendours must lie in the royal palace where the King* stays on his visits to Meknès.

Ritual ablutions must precede the pious Moslem's five daily prayers.

The *médina* is one of the tidiest in Morocco, and though many shops are of the traditional style, others are strictly modern.

As you explore the tortuous labyrinth of the *médina* with its smooth, rounded paving-stones, a thousand sights, sounds and aromas meet you. You'll smell sweet incense, fresh citrus fruit, unseasoned wood from the joiner's shop or the turner's lathe, grilling meat from the cookshop. The streets pass by bubbling fountains graced with coloured faïence and carved cedar. Children carry water away in cans, and bearded old men come out of the mosque after noontime prayers, shuffling and putting on their shoes. The entrance to the mosque is carefully protected from the outside world by a carved cedar screen.

Glittering embroidery hangs in the tiny display window of an equally tiny shop, awaiting buyers. Elsewhere, men and boys talk while sewing away at *jellabas* and caftans. Yet another shop is filled—walls, ceiling, floor, front to rear—with spools of silken thread in all the colours and shades that might

* Departing from traditional usage, the Moroccan sovereign has tended in recent years to adopt the title "king", rather than "sultan".

Health Spas

Though it is possible to enjoy the benefits of Morocco's healthful waters at a distance (in bottles), a cure at the source is much more effective. At Sidi Harazem, between Fez and Taza, a hotel and rental bungalows accommodate those taking the waters for kidney and bladder ailments. The Hôtel des Thermes at Oulmès, south of Meknès, specializes in cures for maladies of the digestive apparatus, arthritis and circulatory problems. The curative waters of Moulay Yacoub, near Fez, are known for their beneficial effects on a variety of troubles ranging from chronic ear, nose and throat afflictions to rhumatism.

conceivably be needed by the weavers and tailors.

Behind tremendous blue-painted doors is an ancient *souk* specializing in blankets and *jellabas*. This is the **Kissaria el Dlala,** always crowded (except on Fridays) with men watching the action as individual blankets and garments are sold at auction.

Along **Rue du Souk en Nejarîn,** a wide variety of shops have been set up in recent times, breaking the solid ranks of carpenters' shops from which the street takes its name.

But here and there you can still find these craftsmen working away with traditional tools at benches completely worn through in some places from centuries of use.

For refreshments, push close to the stand where a boy sells freshly roasted chick-peas in small paper cones, and move off to another stand for a bottled drink. Local people and intrepid tourists with cast-iron stomachs get an even cheaper drink from the itinerant water-seller. His gay, traditional costume from the Rif region and gleaming copper cups are attractive, but somehow his waterbag—a hairy goatskin tightly sewn up with a tube issuing from one of the legs—does little to inspire confidence in the purity of the water.

In your *médina* wanderings, ask a boy to lead you to the doorway of the **Bou Inania médersa.** From there a *gardien* will take over to give you a complete and fact-filled tour of the religious college, built by Abu el Hassan in the 14th century.

The inner courtyard is a treasure-house of intricate detail, much of which has borne up well since the school's construction but is now undergoing restoration. A marble fountain lends the musical sound of running water to the peaceful courtyard. Student cells and a laundry room occupy the arcade off the courtyard. It's possible to climb to the roof of the *médersa* and see the principal monuments from a bird's-eye vantage point. Next-door is Meknès' **grand mosque,** with a green-tiled minaret, and red-tiled roofs and cupolas. This is the largest and most sacred of the dozens of mosques in the city. It's also one of the oldest.

Modern Meknès

Returning to modern Meknès from the old city, take an admiring look at the **Gardens of El Haboul,** in the valley of the Oued Boufekrane. Style in the gardens runs the gamut from highly formal and traditional to very modern and free. Besides an old-fashioned Moorish park, there is a public swimming pool.

Modern Meknès has all the services a visitor may need, as well as cinemas and fairgrounds. One of the best panoramas of the city is yours if you seek out the Hôtel Transatlantique. Near the top of the hillside rising from the riverbed, you can look across to the opposite side of the river to see ancient Meknès ranged along the heights.

Excursions from Meknès

Moulay Idriss

The place where Morocco's "patron" saint (see pp. 13–14) lies buried, is a pleasant, interesting town perched on a hillside above the plateau of Volubilis, 26 kilometres due north of Meknès.

Today Moulay Idriss tumbles down the steep slopes of the Zerhoun massif among olive groves, cacti and clumps of evergreens. It is a microcosm of traditional Moroccan daily life, and a short walk through town will take you past blacksmiths beating at fiery iron, sellers of *kefta* (skewers of mincemeat) sitting patiently by their charcoal grills, "chefs" watching simmering stew kettles and stacking bowls in anticipation

Mother in Moulay Idriss plaits straw baskets in spare moments.

of the lunchtime rush, and all kinds of artisans at work.

Moulay Idriss used to be out of bounds to all non-Moslems, but the rule has been relaxed and tourists are now a common sight in the streets.

As you stroll through town you will have your pick of the local children as guides. Promised a fitting reward of a few coins, the guide will lead you along a winding course through the town to a cul-de-sac on the edge of the promontory. From here you'll have an impressive **view** of the town below, the green-tiled mausoleum of Moulay Idriss and the mountainous countryside around. Your guide will lead you down into the town again, past a striking modern cylindrical minaret, to the entryway of Moulay Idriss's **mausoleum**. A large wooden sign across the passage reiterates the familiar warning: *L'accès n'est pas permis aux non-Musulmans* ("No entry to non-Moslems"). It's easy to console yourself, though, by admiring the huge, ornately coloured and patterned beeswax candles sold in shops near the mausoleum entrance.

Perched on a hill, Moulay Idriss town cradles the saint's tomb.

Baraka

The spiritual power called *baraka* has brought many a Moroccan sultan to the throne, and many a humble but saintly man to the Gates of Heaven. It's that grace, sometimes charismatic, which can make "lesser" men draw back in awe and wonder, a certain power of holiness, blessing and well-being. Every Moroccan *marabout* (holy man) has been a possessor of *baraka*, and expectant pilgrims visit the tombs of these saints hoping to benefit from the blessing of their sanctity. Although not considered a saint, the King of Morocco has *baraka* by virtue of his function as a traditional ruler. In addition, the present king is a *sharif* or descendant of the Prophet, a distinction shared by thousands of Moroccans, but which is all the more propitious when it appertains to the ruler.

Volubilis

From Moulay Idriss it is only a short drive or taxi-ride of 3-odd kilometres to Volubilis, site of the most extensive and impressive Roman ruins in Morocco. The approach to the old regional Roman capital is through rolling hills, orchards and fields.

Volubilis was a flourishing Roman city during the lifetime **43** of Christ. As one of the most important cities in the Mauretania Tingitana province of North Africa, it was a rich and monumental place, and many vestiges of these days of glory survive. Pay the small admission fee, and follow the path down steps adorned with inscriptions and statuary. Little red arrows point out the route of the visitors' path *(chemin des visiteurs)* which winds past temples, baths and a triumphal arch. The most impressive ruins are those of the Forum, Capitol and Basilica which you come to early along, and the houses and palaces which line the Decumanus Maximus, Volubilis' main street. An amateur archaeologist can easily appreciate the importance of Volubilis from the ruins. But everyone, archaeologist or not, can enjoy the dozens of very fine **mosaics** which decorate the floors of houses and public buildings. One of the best is in the Maison au Cavalier, in which the brave and handsome cavalier gazes lovingly at a beauteous maiden. Unfortunately, it is Time rather than the cavalier that ultimately succeeds in ravishing the maiden, for her torso and head have mostly been lost to the ruin brought by the ages.

Volubilis is open to visitors from sunrise to sunset daily. A pleasant, shady outdoor café serves hot and cold drinks, as well as light meals.

Into the Middle Atlas

In the cedar forests of the Middle Atlas are several towns worthy of exploration. **Azrou,** 67 kilometres from Meknès, is the perfect place to get away from city throngs. Built on a hillside in the forest, it is famous not only for its peace and quiet, but also for its carpet-weaving cooperative. The Berber people called Beni M'Guild set up their looms in a central handicrafts market, and you can watch rugs being made as you shop for the finished product.

Ifrane, 71 kilometres from Meknès, is a more active place than Azrou because of its winter-sports facilities, but you needn't visit it only in winter. The many good hotels do a booming business on summer weekends as well (best to reserve in advance) as city folk escape to the cool, fragrant breezes in the mountains.

Mosaic menagerie celebrates the animal wealth of Roman Africa in the monumental city of Volubilis.

FEZ

0   600 m.

0   650 yards

TÉTOUAN, SEBTA (CE

Oued Fès

Route du tour de Fès

Bâb Sidi Bou Jida

Bâb Khoukha

Palais Jamaï

Quartier des Tanneurs

Mosquée des Andalous

Bâb Guissa

Fondouk

P.T.T.

Médersa Misbahiya

Médersa es Sahrij

Tombeaux Mérinides

Médersa el Attarîn

Souk el Attarîn

Mosquée el Karaouine

Hôtel des Mérinides

Place des Seffarîn

Bâb Ftouh

Place en Nejjarîn

Zaouïa de Moulay Idriss

Rue des Teinturiers

Cimetière de Bâb Ftouh

Fondouk

FÈS EL BALI

EL MOKHFIA

Borj Nord

Médersa Bou Inania

Rue du Grand Talaa

Rue du Petit Talaa

Bâb Boujeloud

Place Boujeloud

Bâb el Hadid

Borj Su

Dar Batha (Musée des Arts marocains)

Borj Su

Avenue des Français

Kasba des Cherarda

Av. de la Liberté

Route du tour de Fès

Dar el Beïda

Jardins de Boujeloud

Vieux Méchouar

FÈS EL JEDID

N

Méchouar

Grande rue de Fès el Jedid

Grande Mosquée

Dar el Makhzen (Palais Royal)

Bâb Semmarîn

Av. des Français

Av. du Bou Khareb

Grande rue du Mellah

MELLAH

Place du Commerce

Aguedal

Hôpital

MEKNÈS, RABAT

Boulevard des Saadiens

Bd. des Alaouites

Moulay Youssef

Hôtel de Ville

VILLE NOUVELLE

Av. Mohammed

R. des États Unis

O.N.M.T.

Gare de Tanger-Fès

IFRANE, MARRAKECH, SEFROU, MIDELT

Fez *(Fès)*

Fez, oldest and greatest of Morocco's Imperial Cities, is not really one city, but three. The first city, Fès el Bali, was founded by the Idrissids in the 8th century down in the low land along the Oued Fès. Five hundred years after the founding of Fès el Bali, the Merinids added many jewels of Hispano-Moorish architecture, and built a new city, called Fès el Jédid, next to the old one. Then, during the 20th-century Protectorate, a modern city, the Ville Nouvelle, grew up on higher ground up the valley. A visit to Fez is thus an adventure which takes you deep into Moroccan history, starting from our own time and going back to the early 800s.

Modern Fez

Though you'll spend your days in Fès el Jédid and Fès el Bali, most night-time activities (including sleeping) take place in the modern section of Fez, the Ville Nouvelle. Avenue Hassan II is the axis of the modern town, but many of the most interesting cafés, shops and cinemas are on or near **Avenue Mohammed V.** Though active all day, Avenue Mohammed V is at its circus-like best in the early evening hours. At six or seven o'clock, tradition dictates that the whole town—but especially the young—turn out for a promenade or a glass of mint tea and some conversation. After an hour or so of seeing and being seen, a cosy restaurant is the place to settle down and extend the evening's diversion.

Fès el Jédid

The Merinid town of Fès el Jédid has a city wall of its own. Within it, splendour and the simple life go about their daily business side-by-side. The Royal Palace *(Dar el Makhzen),* where Morocco's king stays when he visits Fez, is almost a town in itself, and a very splendid one at that. Unfortunately it cannot be visited. A richly decorated palace **portal** dominates one side of the Place du Commerce, while on the east side are the crowded streets of the *mellah,* or ancient Jewish quarter. Walk along the shop-lined Grande Rue du Mellah to its end and the great **Bâb Smarîn** (or Bâb Semmarîn) gate. Through the gate, the Grande Rue de Fès el Jédid passes shops and markets on its way to the Vieux Méchouar, once the palace parade-ground.

Just on the other side of Fès el Jédid's eastern wall are the

Jardins de Boujeloud. Bird calls echoing, and the thick stands of bamboo, bring a semi-tropical feeling to the otherwise predictable formal gardens of flowers and spices. An ingenious 13th-century system of channels, pools and dams apportions river water to the various parts of the garden and the city.

Fès el Bali

Before plunging into Fès el Bali, it's imperative to employ a guide, as otherwise it's difficult to find all the places of interest and very easy to become lost. Licensed guides can be hired at the Tourist Office, the *Syndicat d'initiative,* or at any of the larger hotels.

Start from Place Boujeloud. The monumental gate leading into the old *médina* is the **Bâb Boujeloud,** a grand mass of blue-tile stars, flowers and curlicues right in the midst of inter-city buses loading, ironmongers pounding, and costermongers hawking. Two narrow streets lead from the gate into the depths of the **médina:** the Talâa Seghira *(Rue du Petit Talâa)* right before you, and the Talâa Kebira *(Rue du Grand Talâa),* off slightly to your left. Find the latter, the Talâa Kebira, and a few minutes' walk will bring you to the Bou Inania *médersa,* on the right-hand side.

The **Bou Inania médersa,** built in the 1350s, is one of the glories of Hispano-Moorish architecture. As you enter the quiet courtyard leaving the throb of life on the street, the power of the place is bewitching. The dark patina of aged carved plaster harmonizes with the weathered cedarwork. The court is paved in marble, and along the far side a stream of water from the Oued Fès races along a channel. Islamic architects were noted for their

An ideal setting for study of the teachings of the Koran, serene Bou Inania is the finest médersa *(former theological college) in Fez.*

doors, and the several in the courtyard are good examples of how these artists erected what are actually progressions of lintels and arches rising ever higher, impressing the onlooker. Another particularly nice touch in this courtyard is the stalactite work *(muqarnas)* above the windows.

Upstairs are the tiny rooms where the students at the onetime theological college lived. The little slot next to each door was not for mail, but for the students' daily ration of flat bread.

Visitors may not ascend to the upper floors or roof until essential repairs and restoration have been completed.

As you leave the Bou Inania **49**

and enter the busy street, look up to the left at the curious **"clock"** *(carillon de Bou Inania)*, a strange and beautiful contraption with metal discs

Street life in Fès el Bali provides endless fascination. You may see a shirt-maker at work, or a turner with a small bow-driven lathe who works the

Shoppers share streets with delivery donkeys in dyers' quarter.

(originally 13), finely carved wood, and an air of mystery about it. Its maker, its purpose and its method of operation have all been lost in the mists of time.

machine with one hand, steadies it with a foot and holds a chisel in the other hand. Even children have their jobs in the *médina*—you'll come across at least one tiny stand run by junior merchants selling lemonade and sweet pastries.

Don't neglect to peer down passageways and into *souks*

(markets) and *fondouks* (warehouses), for it's in such hidden corners that the basis of *médina* life is found. In one open court are huge sacks of olives to be shared out to retail shops; in another, stacks of brightly painted terra-cotta pots with sheepskin stretched across the mouths await buyers in search of a traditional Moroccan drum.

Continuing along the Talâa Kebira, take some time as you pass through the **Souk el Attarîn** (the perfumers', or spice-merchants' market) to look over the shopkeepers' pharmaceutical and magical wares: tree barks and incense, twigs, roots, charms and potions are all on sale, but it takes a master of the black arts to diagnose illness or to prescribe a magic spell.

Among the traditional druggists' shops are some specializing in souvenirs. A few are set up in beautiful old mansions, and shopping for souvenirs and Moroccan craft items thus gives you the bonus of a tour through a traditional Moroccan house.

Within the *souk*, down a short sidestreet, a minaret covered in white plaster and green faience (green is the Prophet's colour) towers above an ornate gateway. Come up close to the gate (entry, of course, forbidden to non-Moslems) and peer up the steps to the magnificent doors of the prayer room and the glittering chandeliers beyond. This is the **sanctuary of Moulay Idriss II,** builder of Fez and son of the first Moroccan Arab sovereign. The *zaouïa* (monastery) was reconstructed in the 15th century but has been restored more recently. It's a favourite place for Fezzis, especially women, to come for religious inspiration and perhaps a portion of the saint's *baraka.*

At the end of the Souk el Attarîn you approach the richest concentration of beautiful buildings in Fez. Centred on the Karaouine mosque, this is one of the very oldest parts of the city, its foundations dating back a thousand years or more.

The **El Attarîn médersa** (1325) is smaller than its contemporary, the Bou Inania, but equally beautiful. No carved cedar screen separates the courtyard from the student cells. Right in the centre of the courtyard, a marble fountain splashes and plays.

Another *médersa* well worth a visit is just around two corners to the left from the El Attarîn. It's the **Misbahiya médersa** (1346), which has a particularly **51** pretty marble fountain at the centre of its court.

The great jewel of Fès el Bali is undoubtedly the **Karaouine mosque.** First built in the late 9th century on the orders of a woman from Kairouan (Tunisia), the mosque was enlarged and embellished over the centuries. Today it is the most impressive structure in Fez, capable of sheltering thousands of worshippers and dazzling in its decorative richness and detail. Though non-Moslems can't enter the mosque enclosure, the 14 wide doors provide an ample view of the ornate doorways and even a glimpse of the vast interior. The only problem comes from the press of the street throng, which urges along anything in its path. But take some time here, step out of the flow to take a long look. You may also hear of the Karaouine University, which is another name for the same place. From early times Fez has been a centre of Islamic learning, and the Karaouine has been a focal point for both professors and students of religious law and theology.

As you walk around the Karaouine from the El Attarîn *médersa,* you'll come to the pretty "square of the brass- and copper-workers", **Place es Seffarîn.** The banging of hammers on metal is incessant here, and is varied only by the squeal and bubble of red-hot metal being plunged into water to cool it. Samovars, lamps, trays, ewers and even small distilleries sit in every shop, ready to be polished up and carried off to souvenir shops or a waiting customer.

Past the square, a small bridge crosses the Oued Fès. Without crossing, look just upstream from the bridge to the strcet of the dyers *(teinturiers)* —you can tell their shops from the dark stains and fluids everywhere. In modern industry most of the dirty work is done by machines, but in traditional society every part of the manufacturing process had to be done by men. Most accepted the work as God's will, and seemed happy enough.

For a vivid glimpse of medieval manufacturing methods, find your way to the **tanners' quarter** *(quartier des tanneurs)* to see these half-naked workers sloshing the skins in basins of built-up earth, or stacking the reeking hides on to a donkey for shipment to drying places or to the shops of the guild of dyers. The tanners' quarter is

52

Some men, called hafidh, *devote a lifetime to memorizing the Koran.*

not sweet-smelling or uplifting, but it is a true slice of medieval life.

Off in the eastern reaches of Fès el Bali, near the busy work-shops of the potters, is a distinctly different sort of mosque, called the **Andalusian mosque** *(Mosquée des Andalous).* If you come to it by way of the eastern gates in the city walls *(Bâb Ftouh* or *Bâb Khoukha*), it will surprise you by looming above as you round a corner. But if you find your way to el-Andalous through the almost impossible maze of Fès el Bali, you will come to the mosque in its most impressive aspect: a lofty portal at the top of a long flight of steps. It is immediately apparent that the Andalusian mosque is different from the others, though the materials used to fashion its doorway are the familiar tiles, wood and plaster. But there is a special boldness in the design which seems foreign and exotic. The main door, built by an Almo-had sultan in the early 1200s, is all you can see, as entry is reserved for Moslems.

While you are exploring this part of Fès el Bali, take the street to the right of the great door of the mosque to visit the **Es Sahrij** and **Es Sebbayîn médersas,** both well worth investigating.

Wending your way back to Place Boujeloud, be sure to pause at the women's entrance to the sanctuary of Moulay Idriss II. The polychrome and gilt decoration of the **façade** is truly breathtaking, and it alone makes the stop worthwhile, even though you can't go in. The copper plate below the window covered with fancy wrought-iron work had a hole (now covered over) where women could insert an arm to "capture" the saint's blessing, or *baraka.* The saint lies at rest on the other side of the window.

Not far past the sanctuary is Place en Nejjarîn (Square of the Joiners), the centre of cabinet- and furniture-making. The **fountain** built for the joiners is an exquisite, if well-worn, example of Moorish decorative enthusiasm.

The Museum of Moroccan Art *(Musée des Arts marocains)* is a converted mansion called the **Dar Batha,** not far from Bâb Boujeloud. Though you cannot visit the Royal Palace in Fez, the Dar Batha not only gives you a good look at the art of the city but also lets you see how royalty lived a century ago when the palace was built. The large interior garden of the Dar Batha is surrounded by arcades and promenades, and filled with huge trees, spindly cac-

ti 30 feet high, palms, cypresses and jacaranda trees. The ceremonial chambers are now exhibition rooms in which you can scrutinize everything from medieval Arabic astrolabes to local carpets and costumes. To visit, find the caretaker, who will guide you round.

For a look at a similarly gracious palace built around the same time walk past the **Dar el Beïda,** not far from the Dar Batha. Though not officially open to the public, the door is usually ajar and allows you to have a quick glimpse of the layout of gardens and chambers.

Bright-eyed smiles come easily from camera-conscious youngsters.

A Drive Round Fez

The best way to look down on Fez is to drive along the **Route du Tour de Fès** (see map, p. 46), a 16-kilometre circuit surrounding the two older parts of the city and offering commanding views from the heights to the north. As it climbs the slope, the ring road passes the walls to the **Cherarda** *kasba,* surrounded by cemeteries, and soon comes to the **Borj Nord.** This 16th-century fortress now houses an outstand-

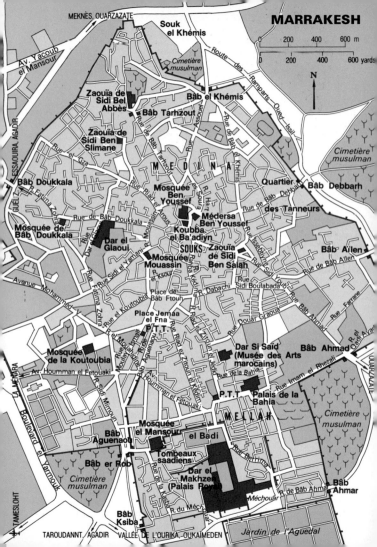

MARRAKESH

200 400 600 m

200 400 600 yards

N

MEKNÈS, OUARZAZATE

Souk
el Khémis

Route des Remparts

Cimetière
musulman

Av. Yacoub
el Mansour

Zaouïa de
Sidi Bel
Abbès

Bâb el Khémis

Bâb Tarhzout

Zaouïa de
Sidi Ben
Slimane

Cimetière
musulman

Rue de Bâb el Khémis

M E D I N A

Bâb Doukkala

Rue el Gza

Mosquée Ben
Youssef

Quartier

Bâb Debbarh

des Tanneurs

Rue de Bâb Dehbaa

GUÉLIZ, ESSAOUIRA, AGADIR

Rue Fatima Zohra

Médersa
Ben Youssef

Mosquée de
Bâb Doukkala

Rue de Bâb Doukkala

Koubba
el Ba'adiyn

Dar el
Glaoui

Mosquée
Mouassin

S O U K S

Zaouïa
de Sidi
Ben Salah

Bâb Aïlen

Rue de Bâb Aïlen

Rue Sidi el Yamani

Rue Riad Zitoun el Kedim

Rue
Sidi Boulabada

Avenue Mohammed

Place de
Bâb Ftouh

R. Dabachi

Rue de la Koutoubia

Place Jemâa
el Fna

Rue Douar Graoua

P.T.T.

Bâb Ahmad

Mosquée
de la Koutoubia

Dar Si Saïd
(Musée des Arts
marocains)

Av. Houmman el Fetouaki

Rue de la Bahia

P.T.T.

Palais de
la Bahia

Rue Imam el Rhezali

Cimetière
musulman

M E L L A H

LA MENARA

Boulevard el Yarmouk

Mosquée
el Mansour

Bâb
Aguenaou

el Badi

Bâb er Rob

Tombeaux
saadiens

Bâb
Ahmar

Cimetière
musulman

Dar el
Makhzen
(Palais Royal)

Rue de Bâb Ahmad

Bâb
Ksiba

Méchouar

R. du Méchouar

TAROUDANNT, AGADIR   VALLÉE DE L'OURIKA, OUKAÏMEDEN

Jardin de l'Aguedal

ing collection of arms from a mammoth 12-ton cannon to a tiny nine-barrelled pistol. Farther along the road is a **viewpoint** and the Hôtel des Mérinides. Stop for a moment here and pick out the landmarks of the city, for when you are in the thick of the *médina* it is impossible to appreciate the city's layout. The ruined tombs of several Merinid sultans stand on a promontory to the east of the hotel.

Now the road winds down into the valley and through olive groves to touch at the Bâb Khoukha and Bâb Ftouh gates before skirting the city walls, passing the abandoned Borj Sud fortress, and returning to the centre of town.

Marrakesh *(Marrakech)*

Heading south, the land becomes drier as you go along. Near Marrakesh the brown foothills give way to a broad plain dominated by what seems to be a mirage: the snow-capped peaks of the High Atlas float above a band of cloud. The mountains are always with you in this southern stronghold, looming majestically on clear days, and fading to an unreal presence when it's misty.

The rugged mountains and arid stretches of plain surrounding Marrakesh are in striking contrast to the green and well-watered town. For almost a thousand years Marrakesh has been an imposing and dominant city, from the time of the Almoravids and Almohads up to the turbulent years of our own century. In fact, the only firm resistance to the rule of Sultan Mohammed V came from Thami el Glaoui, the autocratic and daring Pasha of Marrakesh. The Glaoui, like so many Marrakesh rulers before him, intended to become ruler of all Morocco, but in the end he submitted humbly to the Alaouite sovereign.

Now Marrakesh is the south's commercial centre, a modern city with wide, straight boulevards carrying an easy flow of traffic. Cars, buses, motorbikes and fiacres all move together along **Avenue Mohammed V,** mixing the stench of exhaust fumes with the heavy, heady scent of the orange trees. Café-sitters along the avenue regard tourists with mild curiosity, especially when one of them picks an orange from an ornamental tree. The fruit is bitter, and just for show, and the tasting experiment soon ends...

Near the eastern end of Avenue Mohammed V stands Marrakesh's famed symbol, the **57**

Koutoubia minaret. A towering Moorish monument, it is the finest of the 12th-century Almohad minarets. Each face reflects a different inspiration, almost as though a team of a dozen architects had tried to picture the gates of heaven, and each had worked his own conception into a place on the minaret. A few blue tiles testify to a former splendour of decoration.

The view from the south is particularly imposing, and perhaps the best angle for a photograph. The minaret stands at the end of a long alley with a high ochre wall to the right, a fragrant orange grove to the left. The narrow alley has almost no traffic except the occasional bicycle, so it's the perfect place for youngsters to twist threads which will be used to decorate *burnouses*, *jellabas* and *caftans*. Every day pairs of lads come here to spin their top-like distaffs and the black, blue or gold thread attached.

Approaching Jemaa el Fna square you leave the modern city behind. From block-like Mediterranean-style buildings, the architecture subtly changes to one of blue doors, wrought-iron arabesques on balustrades, shuttered windows. Street life is more rich and varied: here a man daubs oil carefully onto the hubs of his horse-cart while two aged friends nearby squat comfortably in the shade playing draughts (checkers) with bottletops on a makeshift board. Strolling along, a surprise: through a doorway on the right is a cool and shady produce market covered with a lattice of rushes. Above an ancient gate in the medieval city wall, storks survey the activity below from the comfortable sanctuary of their nests. The tink of tinsmiths' hammers sounds from where the masters make metal lamps set with pieces of coloured glass.

"Gathering-place of the extinct" is hardly a suitable name for the liveliest square in Marrakesh, but in fact that is the meaning of Jemaa el Fna. The name dates from the time of a particularly ruthless sultan, who displayed the heads of those who displeased him here in this wide-open space.

Jemaa el Fna is the heart of traditional Marrakesh. Don't let the ranks of taxis and the rows of rickety souvenir stands fool you into thinking that this place is now merely a tourist domain. There are lots

No missing a water-seller's eye-catching costume, even among the scores of stands in Jemaa el Fna.

of tourists—both Moroccan and foreign—but they pour into the square along with the local people to experience this open-air entertainment centre. In the course of a single afternoon and evening you can buy a dress, have a meal, listen to a Moslem preacher (sometimes complete with his own little loudspeaker), watch a man eat fire, or glass, or drink boiling water, have your fortune told, or test your aim in a shooting gallery. Except in the chilliest winter months, a band of brightly dressed black *Gnawa* dancers is always on hand, and will rumble and squeal into action at the approach of any prosperous-looking person. If you've a good eye for bowling, try to knock over several packets of cigarettes at the end of a chalk line drawn on the tarmac. Your prize is—of course—a packet of cigarettes.

The human circus continues and intensifies as darkness falls, and the variety of one-man bands, street-corner orators and itinerant mystics is even greater.

To one side of the enormous irregular "square" small cook-stands sheltered by canvas tarpaulins cater to hungry acrobats and curious tourist alike. Surrounded by benches and shelf-like tables, the local *chef de cuisine* presides over his assortment of dishes, kept warm on charcoal stoves. Table manners are very basic here, and prices are rock-bottom.

After a quarter of an hour amid the swirling throng of Jemaa el Fna, you'll feel like seeking refuge in one of the cafés bordering the square. At a streetside table, children will approach you as they pass, trying their luck: will the magic phrase, *"Un dirham"*, actually produce a windfall coin? If not,

Marrakesh nestles beneath towering Atlas Mountains. Melting snows provide the city's water, cooling breezes keep temperatures moderate.

the attempt is soon forgotten as the child goes about his business. Often children will approach to offer *you* a coin—a franc, mark, or shilling they've been given as a favour by a tourist. They're hoping you can use the coin, and will give them the equivalent in Moroccan money. But you should know that when it comes to working out the rate of exchange, these kids are Morocco's wiliest bankers!

Complete escape from life in the square is possible as some cafés have rooftop sitting areas from which you can watch, but not be in, the ebb and flow of traffic.

61

The Médina

From Jemaa el Fna, various gates and passages lead into the *médina* of Marrakesh. It's best to plan your visit for the morning or early afternoon, because at sundown or thereabouts the whole city seems to empty into the narrow streets of the old quarter, and the press of the crowd is intense. While you don't really need a guide just for a stroll through the *médina*, it's certainly easier to see the interesting buildings if someone helps you. A few dirhams promised to a boy who offers his services will also hold at bay the others who may think of approaching you.

Sooner or later (sooner, if you have a guide) your steps will take you to the *médina*'s highlights. The **Ben Youssef médersa** dates from the 16th century in its present form, and is one of those richly ornate secrets which hide at the end of dark *médina* passageways. Don't neglect the striking ablutions fountain in the courtyard, though it's easy to lose sight of it in the magnificence of wood and plaster arabesques. Nearby is a curious little *koubba* (dome) left from a mosque built in the time of the Almoravids (11th–12th-century).

Though only potentates and prime ministers can generally visit the king's palaces, **Bahia Palace** in the Marrakesh *médina* can be visited by anyone (except when a member of the royal family is at home). A guide leads you to the harem, a beautiful court with rooms for the old-time owner's four legal wives. A small forest of cypress, palms, ivy and creepers is watered by fountains and provided with a shady gazebo, a kind of summerhouse; it was built just for the bewitching ladies and their noble spouse (a grand vizier). The favourite of the four had a sumptuous apartment secluded from the rest, quiet day and night except for the music of a private orchestra. Furnishings and decoration in the palace, from the velvet draperies to the richly painted ceilings, are all as good as new. Not surprising: the grand vizier who built it lived but a century ago.

From the Bahia it's a short but many-cornered way to the **Dar Si Saïd,** another palace built by the same grand vizierial family and now set up to be the Museum of Moroccan Arts *(Musée des Arts marocains)*. The palace rooms are very grand indeed but also somehow very liveable and inviting and, of course, decorated sumptuously. Displays run the gamut of the familiar crafts, and in addition there are some surprises: little wooden sedan-chair boxes fitted on a revolving frame to make a simple Ferris wheel, for lucky children during festivals. For the historically minded, a pictorial display outlines the major architectural monuments of each Moroccan dynasty from the Idrissids to the Alaouites. If you've wondered how the hundreds of pieces of traditional Berber jewellery fit together on a bridal costume, photographs beside the jewellery display show Berber brides in full nuptial regalia.

The delightful **Tombs of the Saadians** *(Tombeaux saadiens)*, once a prominent feature on the outskirts of Marrakesh's *kasba*, were walled up by the magnificent but vengeful Moulay Ismaïl. A passageway has been cut through the wall, though, so visitors can walk among the gardens and hedges of fragrant rosemary to see the exquisite temples where the Saadian imperial families lie buried. Giltwork, Carrara marble and glazed tiles add to the general opulence of the carved cedar and plaster ornamentation. All in all, this is a fitting resting-place for the great Ahmed el Mansour, conqueror of Timbuktu in the late 16th century.

Aguedal and Ménara Gardens

South of the *médina* and the royal palace lies the **Aguedal Garden** *(Jardin de l'Aguedal)*, a vast royal pleasure preserve. Like a deep secret, it must be penetrated ever more deeply to reveal its treasures. First, you pass a crumbling mud wall, to find an olive grove, several miles of it. Water sparkles and gurgles through irrigation ditches, people walk quietly, musing, reading or talking, and young sweethearts make clandestine rendez-vous. Deeper in, past another wall, is a huge irrigation pool. Further still is yet another pool, even larger, with formal gardens behind it, Fruit trees and flowers are everywhere, cultivated or wild, and the occasional renegade fig tree sprouts from the base of a wall, its treats gobbled up by local children almost before they're ripe.

To the west, the **Ménara** is an extensive olive grove. At its centre, an enormous pool reflects perfectly the blue of the sky, and at one end a pavilion provides a vantage-point for gazing at the gardens and the city. The pool and gardens are very old—dating from the time of the Almohads—but succeeding rulers have maintained and improved them. **63**

The City Walls

Marrakesh has grown greatly during the last century, but growth has been in the direction of Guéliz, leaving the ancient city walls uncrowded by new developments. The bare ochre ramparts, crumbling in places but still very formidable, can be seen much as invading armies saw them—less the worry of how to get in.

Without a doubt the best time to tour the walls is at sunrise or sunset, when the sun's long rays show the walls in their richest colour. And the best transport to have is a horse-drawn carriage, easily rented together with driver.

On a half-hour trip through the **Palmeraie** on the north edge of town you will find many photogenic scenes and (maybe) a few camels awaiting you.

Excursions from Marrakesh

Marrakesh is a jumping-off point for trips throughout southern Morocco.

Ourika Valley and Oukaïmeden

(Marrakesh–Oukaïmeden–Marrakesh: approx. 150 km.)
Private car or taxi is the best way to visit the **Ourika Valley,** in the foothills of the High Atlas at the base of DJÉBEL TOUBKAL. Driving into the countryside from the city, there is no dusty semi-desert as you might expect, but lush farmland and orchards on all sides. The fast-running irrigation ditches which lace the land carry the meltwater of Toubkal from Ourika to the city, spreading fertility all along the way.

Ruined fortresses and modest villages at the roadside keep the eye occupied until the Atlas foothills swallow the view. The road winds up and down below tree-topped hills and above dark bottom-land planted with fruit trees, grain and flowers. Springtime is glorious in the Ourika Valley region, for all its orchards are then in bloom; but if you miss this season there will still be lots of greenery and glimpses of village life to assuage curiosity.

At **Tnine el Ourika** close by, a crowded Monday market has much the same character as a county fair. Marketers' vehicles are parked in neat rows down by the river, though in this case the "vehicles" are donkeys rather than cars. "Fodder stations" see to the animals' needs for fuel while shoppers buy the week's groceries and supplies, and catch up on six days' gossip.

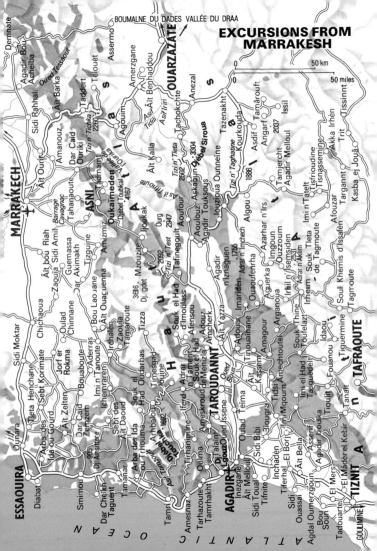

Past DAR CAID OURIKI, the road winds deep into the High Atlas, arriving at **Oukaïmeden,** a well-furnished and very popular winter sports resort. For a view north, as far as Marrakesh on a very clear day, make your way up to **Tizerag** (the last stretch is a quarter-hour on foot). Return to Marrakesh by the same road.

To the Desert's Edge
(Marrakesh–Ouarzazate–Marrakesh: approx. 500 km.)
The P31 road out of Marrakesh leads into the High Atlas and over the 7,400-foot Tizi n'Tichka Pass to the Draa Valley and the town of Ouarzazate. After the grandiose views and forest freshness of the mountains, it descends into an empty plain. This is a region rich in *kasbas.* Part fortress, part palace, the *kasbas* were bases from which petty princes could assert their control over areas large and small. They might play either host or highwayman to the rich caravans passing from the desert through the Atlas on their way to Marrakesh. In this region, life is centred on a string of oases.

At OUARZAZATE, you are on the threshold of the Sahara South. A new town, Ouarzazate was built in 1928 as a garrison post.

Essaouira
Some 75 kilometres due west of Marrakesh on the road to Essaouira lies **Chichaoua,** a carpet-weaving centre with a well-carpeted Sunday market.

Essaouira (175 km. from Marrakesh) is a living memory of pirate days when Spain, Portugal and England vied with Moroccan swashbucklers for control of the coasts. Slightly over 200 years old, the city shows traces of Iberian influence in its forts and towers. The master plan was drawn up by a Frenchman who was a prisoner of the sultan, and so the jumble of tortuous streets normally found in a Moroccan *médina* is slightly more orderly here. An attractive beach on the south side is served by several good hotels and restaurants. At the west—town—end of the beach is the fishing harbour and the *skala* (battery) left from pirate times. A main street runs straight through town from the customs house near the fishing harbour to the Bâb Doukkala, and once you've walked past all the shops, through the gates and under the arches along the thoroughfare, you've experienced a good deal of Essaouira's daily life. At Bâb Doukkala, when the fishing boats come in, there are little stalls on hand to fry up the catch.

Taroudannt

A single glimpse of Taroudannt, 225 kilometres from Marrakesh, can tell you its whole history. Surrounded by olive groves, citrus orchards and green fields, it is at the centre of the rich Sous (or Souss) plain, well-watered from the High Atlas slopes. At a time when coastal towns were open to naval attack, Taroudannt's inland location and high tawny walls made it the natural and impregnable capital of the region. The gigantic fortifications have been kept in good repair, and still provide the most striking attraction of the town. Within them, dusty squares and market-places, almost unaltered, could provide the backdrop for a Humphrey Bogart film.

After the walls, Taroudannt's *souks* are its main attraction. The artisans here are justly famed for their stone carvings, though a 200-pound souvenir is hardly the thing for the modern air traveller. There are smaller items, however, and a moment's admiration of the craftsmen's work provides a memory which weighs nothing.

Palm-trees keep the desert alive, casting patches of welcome shade and providing sweet dates for food.

Agadir

Nothing could be more modern than Agadir, some 240 kilometres from Marrakesh. Although the name comes from the 16th-century *agadir* (fortress) on a hilltop to the north, the city itself is all new. A fearsome earthquake in 1960 completely levelled the old town. The new city, built on a safe, earthquake-free site, is devoted to the rich commerce of the Souss and the entertainment of foreign sun-seekers.

White buildings, bold, modern architecture and bright sunlight give visitors a dazzling first impression, but the real wonder of Agadir reveals itself when you first put on your bathing clothes and go down to the beach. This great swath of fine-grained sand is a huge crescent some 10 kilometres long and up to 400 yards wide. The slope of the beach in the water is gradual, making it good for small children, and yet the surf farther out is good enough to warrant the use of a surfboard.

A good number of luxury hotels have been built along the edge of the beach. Al-

Traditional lifestyle continues little changed in super-modern Agadir. **69**

though construction continues apace, there remain a few cool and shady groves of eucalyptus trees.

Beach life occupies most of every tourist's day in Agadir, and cafés near the beach provide necessities. In late afternoon and evening the centre of activities moves back into town, to open-air cafés, bistros, souvenir and handicraft shops, and the bars and nightclubs of the large hotels. Bars, which stay open past midnight, are the best place for night-owls (the cafés begin to close soon after 10 o'clock).

Tiznit and Goulimine

The mountains of the Anti-Atlas form a barrier south of Agadir, blocking it from the Sahara. Much of the ancient caravan traffic skirted the mountains. The detour was good for the towns along the way, and made Tiznit and Goulimine what they are today.

Bring along your childhood conception of a fortified desert oasis, for that is exactly what **Tiznit,** 92 kilometres from Agadir, turns out to be. A crenellated red wall surrounds the town, and palm trees spread their frond umbrellas here and there. Though a few shops and hotels aim their services at

the tourist trade, most of the town exists for the townspeople alone. You shop alongside them in the interesting little jewellers' *souk,* the place to look for heavy old Berber brooches and pins.

Goulimine, 200 kilometres from Agadir, is at the very edge of the Sahara, and desert life

For all its harshness, the desert can be exceptionally beautiful. Camels provide transport, food, clothing, fuel for rugged desert-dwellers.

has formed its character. Dusty Land Rovers parked here and there attest the citizens' desert preoccupation, but the true means of desert transport are grouped together in the mar-ket-place every Saturday. Not just camels are bought and sold here on Saturdays, though. The dramatically draped "blue men" of the desert, who still make the trek through the **71**

Sun, shade, simple decoration: the basics of an unassuming artistry.

burning sands to Timbuktu, have traded everything from gold to gadgets here, and still do. Pick up a few yards of the indigo-dyed cloth out of which they make their garments, and as the dye bleeds on your skin, you will discover how the blue men got their curious name.

Apart from the colour and commotion of market-day, Goulimine has a small collection of eating-places, some shops, and an old *ksar*, or stronghold. The *moussem* (festival) of Sidi M'Hamed Benamar, in early June, brings tribesmen out of the desert for worship, gatherings and games.

Tangiers *(Tanger)*

At the northern tip of Morocco and at the meeting-point of Africa and Europe, Tangiers has always held something of a special position in Moroccan history. The Phoenicians set up a trading station here, and later the Romans founded the town of Tingis, which lent its name to their province of Mauretania Tingitana. It was brought to England as part of the dowry of Catherine of Braganza, the bride of Charles II. It became Moroccan again in 1681.

During the years of the Protectorate (see p. 18), Tangiers had a special status. It was an "international zone", governed by a committee of diplomats, and this peculiar arrangement—together with the city's special privileges—attracted all kinds of adventurers. Though Tangiers today is as much a part of Morocco as is Rabat or Marrakesh, it still keeps an international flavour because of the heavy tourist traffic which crosses the straits and lands here before heading south to the interior.

A visit to Tangiers and northern Morocco requires a switch in languages. During the Protectorate, northern Morocco was governed by Spain, and the predominance of Spanish over French still survives. Though many Tangerines (as the inhabitants are called) will be able to speak to you in both French and Spanish as well as Arabic, chances are you'll hear *buenos días* rather than *bonjour*.

The Heart of Town

At the centre of the modern city is Place de France and Boulevard Pasteur. Cafés and restaurants, bookstores and travel agencies are all within a few blocks of the square. The **73**

At the crossroads of Atlantic and Mediterranean, Europe and Africa, fabled, cosmopolitan Tangiers still exudes a sense of intrigue.

terrace just out of Place de France along Boulevard Pasteur has a fine view of the harbour and the Spanish mainland, and is a favourite gathering-place in the evenings for tourist and Tangerine alike.

The *médina*, covering a hillside, is a maze of narrow streets, passages and blind alleys. As it is not all that large, perhaps the best way to explore it is simply to lose yourself. As you wander about looking for a familiar landmark, *médina* life both

secret and obvious will be revealed to you. Two traditional centres to look for are the Grand Socco (great *souk*, or market), officially called Place du 9 Avril 1947, and the Petit Socco. The Grand Socco, on the edge of the *médina* proper, is now the terminus for city buses, and has a large taxi rank. The **Petit Socco,** within the *médina*, is a pleasant open space with several cafés, and is a natural theatre in which to watch the drama of market life.

The Kasba

At the top of the hill above the *médina*, the *kasba* of Tangiers seems impregnable from land or sea. It is no surprise that the great Alaouite sultan, Moulay Ismaïl, chose to build himself a palace behind the batteries of cannon installed on the walls. Today the palace houses two museums.

Walking along Rue Riad Sultan, a large unmarked doorway opens on a pretty courtyard with ivy- and vine-covered trellises, orange trees and twittering birds. This is the **Sultan's Garden,** part of Moulay Ismaïl's palace. Another small garden next to it has banana plants and a gigantic triple-trunk fig tree. From here you enter the palace of **Dar el Makhzen.**

The beautiful interior court, surrounded by plump marble columns, is the centre of the palace's **Museum of Moroccan Arts.** Doorways and passages lead from here into the exhibition rooms where you can gaze to your heart's content at such treasures as illuminated Korans, fine textiles, delicate wood and metal work, Berber carpets, jewellery and a ceramics collection. The adjoining Antiquities Museum is concerned with aspects of Tangiers' history.

You can leave the palace by the elegant treasury, **Bit el Mal;** several rooms with a balcony overlook the *méchouar* (parade ground). Things were pretty basic in Moulay Ismaïl's day, as you will realize upon seeing the gigantic wooden strongboxes of the treasury, which were once filled with gold and precious gems.

Cross the *méchouar* to the observation point which looks north from this high and advantageous location. Here you have the best view of the harbour and the straits.

Excursions from Tangiers

Chaouen

(Chéchaouen / Chefchauen / Xauen)

One of the most memorable excursions that you can make from Tangiers is to the town of Chaouen, 120 kilometres away, high in the Rif mountains.

The way will lead through TÉTOUAN, some 60 kilometres south. Despite its historical importance as a major settlement area for Moorish exiles from late 15th-century Spain, expelled after the Christian Reconquest, and its subsequent reputation as a nest of pirates,

Tétouan is of little interest to today's tourists.

Chaouen comes as a surprise. From its dramatic location with rocky mountain peaks and precipitous defiles at its back, this little town surveys the hills around and the valleys below. A quick look at the town reveals its history, for here a typical Moroccan *médinu* co-exists with a classic Spanish town *plaza* complete with topiary arches, grape arbours and tiled benches around a central fountain. The town hall and church are also here on the Plaza Mohammed V.

A shady spot at Chaouen's market, ideal for chatting to old friends. Right: tile patchwork in Asilah, a fine sample of local styles.

But today it is Islam that rules in Chaouen, the Spaniards having left in 1956 after an occupation of 36 years. Though the red tile roofs and similar Spanish touches remain, what you will remember of Chaouen is its Moroccan ambience. Up from **Plaza el Makhzen,** with its painted arcades and small shops, is a centuries-old **kasba,** recently restored. Its gardens, planted with palm-trees and flowers, are a haven of tranquillity.

Souks and *bazaars* abound in the *médina*, offering the products of local carpet factories, and also polished stones gathered from the surrounding hills.

The hinterland of Chaouen provides impressive **views:** steep green foothills covered with pasture and fields, orchards and small, white, tin-roofed houses surround the town itself, except for where the mountains rise too steeply for building or cultivation.

Asilah and Lixus

Forty-five kilometres south of Tangiers along the road to Rabat there lies the charming town of **Asilah.** Just slightly off the main road and right on the shore, Asilah is almost the picture-postcard Atlantic fishing port, complete with an impressive *kasba.* Though now thoroughly Moroccan, the town was captured by the Portuguese in 1471 (they left their architectural mark in its walls and bastions). Foreign occupation—the Portuguese were succeeded by the Spaniards—was to last some 200 years. Around the turn of the present century, Asilah was the stronghold of a devil-may-care Moroccan brigand named Raissouli, who built himself a palace within the *kasba* walls.

But there is more to Asilah than its sights: just outside the town walls, right down by the sea, several small seafood restaurants are set up, with tables outside by the street and in a garden setting. The daily catch, fresh in from the boats, is served up for lunch with a minimum of ceremony and a maximum of flavour, and prices are quite reasonable. No one who is in on the secret passes Asilah without stopping to have lunch.

From Asilah, it is only 38 kilometres further to the ruins of ancient **Lixus,** one of the oldest cities in Morocco. The first settlement here, a Phoenician trading-post, may have been established as early as the 11th century B.C. In any case, it was an important town while Morocco was part of the Roman province of Mauretania

Tingitana, and it grew rich on shipping salt and fish to the capital city. The remains of the fish-salting factories are right down by the highway. Temples, baths, and a theatre make up the acropolis, at the top of the hill.

The valley of the river Loukos, which flows close by, is thought to have been the site of the Garden of the Hesperides, famous from Greek mythology for its trees that bore golden apples.

Unexpected display of modern wall art provides surprise in Asilah.

What to Do

Shopping

The *souks* and *médinas* of Morocco's Imperial Cities come to you straight out of the *Arabian Nights*. The best time to explore them is during the day, however, and preferably shops remain open on Friday, the Moslem holy day.

Shops in the *souks* are everyday business enterprises, but the weekly market in each vil-

Hang it or stack it, but get it out where customers can see it; storeroom and showroom are one.

before early evening brings the heavy crowds. Shops open usually from about 8 a.m. to noon and 3.30 to 7 p.m., except Sundays (closed all day). A few lage and town brings a very different element to Moroccan commercial life. Here are some of the most lively and interesting markets:

Agadir: Saturday and Sunday

Chaouen: Thursday

Goulimine: Saturday (camel market)

Marrakesh: Thursday (camel market)

Taroudannt: Friday

Tiznit: Thursday and Friday

Best Buys

First on most visitors' lists in Morocco is morocco **leather,** fine-grained and buttery-soft, used to cover books, desk utensils, portfolios and a myriad of other articles.

Goods made of sturdier leather are also big-sellers: poufs, satchels, valises, wallets, handbags and *babouches* (slippers).

Silver **jewellery** is attractively florid, and not overly expensive if of modern make. Antique Berber jewellery of silver, amber and coral fetches a pretty high price, but is strikingly beautiful.

Textile products are favourites, too. Women will want to pick up at least one *caftan*, plain or fancy, for use as a nightgown, casual dress or even as a party dress. Men may find a *burnous* a bit cumbersome, but a traditional hooded black cape is not only practical and handsome, but very dramatic as well.

If transport is no problem, consider one of the brilliant **copper trays** with hammered designs which, along with a small folding stand, make useful and attractive little tables.

Squat, Oriental **teapots** used for infusing mint are made of silver, pewter and even aluminium, and so you can choose one which fits both your needs and your budget.

Moroccan **carpets** generally have a looser weave of larger knots, and a deeper pile, than the more familiar handmade pieces. Patterns are not so intricate as Persian or Turkish ones. But Moroccan carpets are certainly sturdy and attractive, and compared to the more prestigious products are also very reasonably priced. They are sold in all major cities but are made mostly in the smaller towns,

Prices are lowest in the crowded little souk *stores, where bargaining skills can be finely honed.*

where you will get a better price and selection. Often the artisans band together in a co-operative to set quality standards and prices. If this is the case, prices will be marked and sellers inflexible; shopkeepers in *bazaars* may be open to haggling.

Bargaining
In an economy where many products are handmade, each item has a different value depending on the quality of workmanship it shows. Bargaining is thus a way of determining the proper price, not simply a way for a shopkeeper to get more money from one customer than from the next. To get the best price, though, you must get to know the market by browsing in several shops and asking the prices of comparable pieces. In general, final prices in Morocco should be quite low compared to first prices.

If bargaining annoys you, an easier and less time-consuming way is simply to find something you like and decide what it's worth to you. If an attractive pouf or suitcase looks to be well-made and would cost the equivalent of 200 dirhams at home, you might decide that you should pay between 75 and 100 dirhams for it here. Ask the price: if the shopkeeper quotes

you a price of 80 dirhams, you have a bargain; if he says the price is 150, offer him 75, and you will end up at 100. If he doesn't come down to your price, there is no shame in walking away when you've bargained and have been unable to agree upon a price. Deciding what an item is worth to you is a method guaranteed to avoid dissatisfaction.

Sports

Beaches and Swimming
Morocco has a 1,200-mile-long coastline with many outstanding beaches. Those near Rabat are particularly beautiful: **Témara,** south of the city, and the **Plage des Nations,** north of the city, are both favoured by knowledgeable beach-lovers in the summer months. Others all along the Atlantic coast are equally suitable. The magnificent beach at **Agadir** may be Morocco's finest; and of all those on the Atlantic, it is the only one well protected against the dangerous problem of undertow. Anywhere on the Atlantic it is advisable not to venture out of your depth. If an undertow catches you, it can sweep you out to sea in a matter of minutes.

Morocco's Mediterranean **83**

beaches are pleasant and warm, and generally free of the threat of undertow. The shores backed by the Rif mountains are just now being developed as resorts. Some of the best hotel and restaurant facilities are immediately south of **Sebta** (Ceuta): you could also explore the possibilities at **Cabo Negro, Smir-Restinga, M'diq** and **Taïfor.**

Golf

In Morocco, golf is a royal sport: King Hassan II takes great interest in the game. Rabat has two 18-hole courses and one 9-hole course, with luxurious clubhouse facilities. Other 18-hole courses can be played at Mohammedia and Marrakesh. Tangiers, Meknès and Casablanca each have a 9-hole course. The links are open year-round.

Fishing

The coasts, lakes and rivers offer limitless possibilities to the fisherman, whether his choice is deep-sea fishing, surf-casting, underwater spear-fishing, or angling in mountain lakes and streams. Depending on your luck and skill you may come up with a two-pound bass or a sixty-pound *mérou*. Season dates and permits are available from: Direction des Eaux et Forêts, Ministère de l'Agriculture, Rabat. Alternatively, each town of any size has a Service des Eaux et Forêts (Waters and Forests Service) where you can obtain information and permits. Local fishing clubs can be of help in procuring rental equipment and information.

Sailing

Sailing clubs in Tangiers, Rabat, Mohammedia, Casablanca, Agadir and other coastal towns are on hand to assist foreign sailing enthusiasts with help and advice in exploring the inlets and bays of the Moroccan coasts.

Riding

A very active riding federation links the country's many riding clubs. Mounts can often be hired and a ride along the beach or into the Moroccan countryside is an unforgettable experience. For information, and possible short-term membership, contact: Fédération d'Equitation, Dar es Salam, Rabat, or the local *Cercle Hippique, Etrier,* or *Club Equestre* (riding clubs are variously known by these names).

Whatever your favourite beach pursuit, beware of hot Moroccan sun!

Hunting

The tourist is the most pampered hunter in Morocco: he has his own 295,000-acre hunting reserve at Arbaoua, near the coast south of Larache. When you show the officials in charge your foreign hunting licence, they will sell you a non-renewable 30-day permit for the reserve. Moderately priced insurance is compulsory and available on the spot. No rifled-barrel guns are allowed —only shotguns. The season usually extends from October to February. Hare, wild boar, and duck are hunted.

Other, slightly smaller, hunting zones can be explored near the towns of Essaouira, Ouezzane, Oulmès, Mamora, Meknès and Marrakesh. The season runs from late September to the first part of March. The Ministry of Tourism should have all the details, or you can contact: Fédération Royale de Chasse, 36, boulevard Mangin, B.P. 724, Rabat.

Skiing

Despite the widely held conception of Morocco as only a camel caravan country, skiing possibilities do exist in the Middle and High Atlas and Rif ranges—snow conditions permitting (some years snow is bountiful, others not). Oukaïmeden, near Marrakesh, and Ifrane, near Meknès, are well situated and equipped to look after all the needs of winter sport enthusiasts. On weekends in winter, hotel reservations are advisable.

Nightlife

Early evening is promenade time in all Moroccan cities and towns, and everyone turns out to see and be seen. Promenaders take turns at café tables, resting and watching the parade until they feel like joining in again. Every cinema has an animated crowd in front, whether the film be in French, Arabic or another language. For some spots, like Marrakesh's Jemaa el Fna square, evening brings an increase in the number and variety of open-air entertainments. The action starts to die down as midnight approaches.

Major hotels, in conjunction with local Syndicats d'initiative, schedule evenings of folklore and folk dancing, and the somewhat un-Moroccan but nevertheless highly interesting belly-dance is often the centrepiece of the show. Small clubs in some cities have disco music for dancing, while the bars of the large hotels are good places to make new friends and talk over the day's adventures.

Marrakesh, Mohammedia and Tangiers each has its gambling casino, aglitter with socialites and the tempting but generally illusory prospect of increasing your holiday funds.

Many tourists find that the best way to finish off a day is with a short stroll to a congenial *bistrot* (café-bar), and a relaxed, unhurried evening meal.

Folklore

Though modernization has come to Morocco, its rich traditional way of life is still vigorous and intact.

The Rijel Zuraq—the famous "blue men" of the desert—still depart with brave ceremony for their annual

An experienced grip on a dangerous foe turns him into a friend.

caravan into the Sahara. At various times during the year, *moussems* (religious festivals) bring tribal and family groups from all over the country to a saint's tomb for days of devotion, merriment and folk entertainments. Several spectacles are worthy of special consideration. The King's Friday procession to the mosque, accompanied by a resplendent guard of honour, is one of the oldest and most fascinating of Moroccan pageants. It takes place in Rabat—but only when conditions of weather, diplomacy and court life are favourable. The daily changing of the guard at the Tomb of Mohammed V in the same city (the hour is variable) is another sight not to be missed, if possible.

Folk dancing is a big part of any popular festival or religious holiday. Most famous is the *guedra,* performed by veiled Berber girls in the far southern reaches of the country. Though hardly an exciting "dance of the seven veils", it is strange and mysterious: the dancer is seated throughout, and heavily veiled, and entrances her audience by the undulating movements of arms and hands.

The liveliest and most rhythmic Moroccan dancers are not originally Moroccan. You'll

recognize the *Gnawa* dancers by their black-and-white costumes decorated with seashells, and by the quick and exciting beat of their drums and pulse of their chanting. One group is based quasi-permanently in Marrakesh's Jemaa el Fna square, and others appear whenever a festival promises to

Mock-warriors hurtle forward on Arab steeds in a rousing fantasia.

provide an appreciative audience.

The finest of all Moroccan folklore is the breathtaking *fantasia*, a display of brilliant precision horsemanship. Imagine yourself seated in an audience outdoors, with a band of horsemen in flowing robes thundering down upon you, long rifles twirling in the air, war cries echoing above the thunder of hooves. Then all at once—seemingly without a **89** central command—they all stop dead in their tracks at the edge of the crowd with a crackling of dozens of rifles, retreating afterwards as quickly as they came. Moroccans love *fantasias*, and you will probably get the chance to witness one at any large festival or important *moussem*. You shouldn't miss it.

Festivals and Moussems

Holidays and festivals are a big part of Moroccan life. Largest and most fascinating festivals are the *moussems*, gatherings held in honour of a saint. These are usually colourful annual events which draw crowds of different sizes, from a small group of villagers making a trip to a local saint's tomb to

Moussems are a time for music-making; the medieval Moslem instrument called el-oud *was adopted by Europe's troubadours as the lute.*

a huge convention of thousands of people who set up camp at a holy spot and entertain themselves with day-and-night shows of dancing, juggling, acrobatics, storytelling, and *fantasias*. Though non-Moslems are not allowed to approach a saint's tomb in most cases, everyone is welcome to participate in the festive merry-making, whether for an hour, a day, or a whole week.

The major religious holidays of Islam are dated according to the lunar calendar, which means the dates move, coming almost two weeks sooner each year by our system. See PUBLIC HOLIDAYS in the Blueprint section of this book for details on holidays.

Major Festivals

End of March	*Casablanca*	Theatre festival
Early May	*Essaouira*	Moussem of Zaouïa el Kettania
May/June	*Meknès*	Regional fair
May/June	*Fez*	Regional fair
May/June	*Marrakesh*	National folklore festival
Early June	*Goulimine*	Moussem of Sidi M'Hamed Benamar
June	*Casablanca*	Moussem of Sidi Moussa
July	*Chaouen*	Moussem of Outa Hammou
Early August	*Témara (Rabat)*	Moussem of Sidi Lahcen
August	*Rabat*	Moussem of Dar Zhirou
August	*Ourika (Marrakesh)*	Moussem of Sitti Fatma
Late August	*Essaouira*	Moussem of Sidi Mogdoul
Late August	*Tiznit*	Moussem of Sidi Ali ou Moussa
Early September	*Fez*	Moussem of Sidi Ahmed el Bernoussi
Early September	*Marrakesh*	Moussem of Sidi Abdalhak ben Yasin
Mid-September	*Marrakesh*	Moussem of El Guern
Mid-September	*Marrakesh*	Moussem of Sidi Bonatinane
September	*Moulay Idriss (Meknès)*	Moussem of Moulay Idriss Zerhoun
Late September	*Agadir*	Moussem of Aït Baha
November	*Marrakesh*	Regional fair

Wining and Dining

Simple elegance and abundance are the qualities that most often characterize traditional Moroccan cuisine. In some Arab lands even the salads come heavily freighted with fiery pepper, but in Morocco the surprises are more often sweet than hot.

Where to Eat

The Protectorate had a great influence on the restaurant scene in Morocco's Imperial Cities, and today it is a simple matter to find an excellent French restaurant in any urban area. The menu you read and the service you receive will follow the French tradition. In the north, Spanish cuisine and restaurants are also common, thanks to former Spanish presence in this part of the country. In Tangiers, Rabat and Marrakesh you may also come across Chinese, Vietnamese, Italian and other places to dine.

The large international hotels always have a balanced menu of the familiar and the exotic, to please all comers. Local specialities such as *couscous* are found alongside well-known dishes almost everywhere.

In the *médinas*, cook-shops serve very simple fare at rock-bottom prices under very questionable sanitary conditions.

For breakfast, a snack or a light lunch, every city and town has French-inspired outdoor cafés, and in the larger cities American-style lunch-counters have begun to make their appearance.

Cafés are an integral part of the Moroccan way of life. Ideal for a coffee or a quick snack, they are also the place to make friends.

Breakfast

Whereas the traditional Moroccan breakfast consists of mint tea, toasted bread and a handful of olives, city-bred Moroccans begin their day *à la française*, with coffee and a pair of *croissants* or other pastries brought fresh from the local pastry-shop. As often as not, breakfast is taken at an outdoor café table. A basket of *crois-* **93** *sants* is left on the bar for customers to help themselves; when the time comes to pay you indicate to the waiter how many you've taken. In a hotel, the standard "tourist" breakfast includes one *croissant*, one bun or sweet roll, jam and butter, with coffee, tea or hot chocolate. It's dangerous to eat much more as the midday meal may be an elaborate affair… followed by a siesta.

Lunch and Dinner

Lunchtime is between 12 noon and 3 p.m., and dinner is served between about 7 and 9 p.m.

A formal Moroccan-style meal is likely to follow the pattern soup – *bstilla* – *couscous* – dessert, though you will normally find a single dish sufficient for your needs.

Soups

Best-known of Moroccan soups is *harira*, a thickish, savoury soup made with lentils, onions, mutton and veal and tomatoes. Special varieties are favoured on dinner tables at Ramadan, but you will find *harira*—it's virtually a generic term for thick soup—offered in restaurants all year round.

Bstilla *(bastela, pastilla)*

Bstilla is the favourite local delicacy, not nearly so common on menus as *couscous* because it takes a great deal of time and labour to prepare. First the pigeons are cooked, and then the meat is spread in layers of paper-thin *ouarka* (flaky pastry) along with saffron, almonds and sugar. Baked to a delightful crispness, the finished *bstilla* is the triumph of Moroccan cuisine.

Other dishes involving flaky pastry are more common. *Briouats*, for instance, are small pillows of thin pastry dough filled with *kefta* (spiced finely-chopped meat), rice, almonds, brains, sausage, fish—almost anything. These are then deep-fried quickly and served hot. *Rghaïfs*, though difficult to order because of their unpronounceable name, will reward the effort. Stuffings of many kinds are tucked within the folds of thin, fried pancakes and served hot, making a delicious prelude to a more substantial main course.

Couscous

It's virtually impossible to visit Morocco without encountering the local staple *couscous*, at least once. It consists of tiny, steamed savoury semolina pellets topped with stewed vegetables and meat. Every chef has his or her own private recipe, and at one time or another every vegetable has accompanied the succulent pieces of mutton on top of the mound of *couscous* grains. One version features a roasted sheep's head—though you will not encounter this one unless you look for it. Moroccans are trained from birth to eat *couscous* politely and deftly with the fingers of the right hand: a raisin, chick-pea, or morsel of meat is scooped up with some *couscous* and in a few gentle rolls of the fingers has been converted into a perfectly spherical bite-size morsel of food, which is then popped into the mouth. Unpractised foreigners are always provided with knife, fork and spoon.

Other Main Dishes

You will probably have to wander into the hungry crowd at a *moussem* to encounter a Moroccan *méchoui*. Only at outdoor festivals are the conditions right for digging a pit, filling it with charcoal, and then roasting a whole lamb over the slow coals. Service at such a rough-and-ready restaurant may not be of the most elegant, but the aroma alone will easily make up for that.

You need not wait for a *moussem* to have roast meat, for charcoal-broiled *kebab* (skewers of meat) are found everywhere. You may find them made of lamb, beef, liver or heart. Those sensitive to the thought of eating underdone meat should specify the *kebab* "*bien cuit*" (well done).

Kefta, minced (ground) meat rissoles made with savoury spices, are served in a variety of ways. Delicious as grills, they are also cooked with fried eggs and hot chili peppers to make an attractive, if incendiary, dish.

Chicken is a frequent sight on Moroccan tables and may be simply roasted, served on top of a small mountain of *couscous*, or stewed in many appealing ways. For instance, the famous Moroccan *poulet au citron* is made with sweet spices and the lemon peel pickled for several weeks in brine, and the zest of the lemon contrasts very nicely with the richness of the chicken. Another, and an even more exotic, chicken dish is made with prunes and a generous sprinkling of almonds sautéed in butter, and roasted sesame seeds.

The Moroccan stew is called a *tajine*, after the earthenware pot in which it is traditionally prepared. The best restaurants will still serve the dish in the pot with a conical lid, though it is doubtful that the chef really cooked it the traditional way by burying it within a charcoal fire **95** in the ground. There is never any agreement as to what should be cooked in *tajine:* tomatoes, marrow (squash), peas and beans, carrots, aubergines (eggplants), and every other vegetable of the Moroccan market has had its turn in the pot, joining pieces of lamb, veal or beef. You may see a *tajine* made with fish identified by the name *hout* on some menus.

Mouth-watering sweet pastries make tasty treats any time. A hearty dish of couscous *(right) satisfies the most ravenous of appetites.*

Fish and Seafood

A very long coastline and numerous inland lakes and streams provide a good variety of fish for the Moroccan table. Mullet, dorado, shad and sea perch head the list. Fish can be used in a *tajine* or *couscous*, but is more often prepared alone as a main course. It may be simply grilled or poached or prepared by a more complex rite of marinating, baking or stewing.

Moroccan waters also yield a fine selection of seafood *(fruits de mer)*, especially octopus *(poulpe)* and squid *(calamar)* served deep-fried, and baby eels the size of matchsticks. The eels are sautéed in butter and garlic, and are delicious.

Salads

Though foreign influence has brought the simple *salade verte* (green salad) to Morocco, the traditional salads usually require tomatoes, parsley, lemon juice, olive oil, and even a pinch of the ubiquitous cumin. Ingredients may be served raw, or cold after having been cooked together.

Desserts and Fruit

Moroccans undeniably have a sweet tooth. Honey is a major ingredient in many familiar desserts: *briouats*, little pillows of ultra-thin pastry, appear as a salty main course, but as a sweet the *briouats* are stuffed with honey and almonds. *Griouches*, twisted strips of honeyed pastry dough baked and sprinkled with sesame seeds, are popular as the last course at dinner, and also as a snack at *moussems* and in *souks*.

Best-known of the local after-dinner treats is *kaab el ghzal*, meaning gazelle's horns —small horn-shaped delicacies with a filling of almond paste flavoured with orange-flower water. A few of these make the perfect companion for your post-prandial cup of coffee.

If you have a really sweet tooth, search the menu for stuffed dates *(dattes farcies)*, which in the classic preparation means best-quality dates stuffed with a paste of toasted almonds, sugar and orange-flower water.

Fruit is a delight to the unaccustomed visitor from the north. Oranges, peaches, figs, dates, apricots—buy them succulently fresh from roadside or market stalls, in season.

Drinks

Islam forbids the use of intoxicating beverages, and strict Moslems will touch nothing stronger than mineral water or mint tea in order to keep within the rules. But those who enjoy wine with a meal and those who abstain live and dine peaceably together.

The French legacy of wine-making in Morocco helps to enhance dining. In the major cities, even small and modest restaurants will have a few good local wines to choose from, and the better places will have quite a varied selection. Favourites of long standing are *cabernet* (red and rosé), *valpierre* (red and white), *vieux pape* (red), *oustalet* and *boulaouane* (rosé and white) and *guerrouane* (rosé).

98 Many other labels will come

to your notice, and you should not miss a chance to do some tasting.

French influence is also responsible for the large assortment of aperitif wines found in bars and cafés, some of which are bottled in Morocco. Stronger drinks such as whisky, gin, rum, vodka and brandy (including Cognac) can be ordered in the larger hotels and better-stocked cafés.

Beer is brewed and bottled in Morocco, and is readily available in cafés as well as restaurants. You may find the local product somewhat different from what you're used to, in which case you should ask for one of the internationally known brands brewed under licence in Morocco.

Prices of drinks are moderate, particularly if you drink what the Moroccans drink—mineral water, mint tea, various soft drinks.

You'll see espresso coffee machines everywhere, though the product usually turns out to be somewhat tasteless.

Black tea is available, but tends to be rather weak.

Mint Tea—A Ceremony

No visit to a Moroccan home could be complete without the friendly hocus-pocus of mint tea. A squat and curvy pot of silver, pewter, aluminium or enamel is filled with boiling water, then emptied. Green tea and mint are jammed into the pot together with a small amount of boiling water which is swished around the pot and then poured away. Sugar is now added and the pot filled with boiling water. This is allowed to stand for a few minutes; the teapot is then held high and a glass filled and the contents poured back into the pot. Then a further glass is filled which is tasted for sweetness, sugar is added accordingly and the tea, finally, is served. (Needless to say, the host's good aim with the boiling liquid is crucial to the success of the ceremony.)

Though you may not have the chance to visit a Moroccan home, you can still enjoy the tea in any café, without, alas, the touch of the traditional ceremony.

To Help You Order...

Could we have a table for..., please?
Do you have a set menu?

Pouvons-nous avoir une table pour..., s'il vous plaît?
Avez-vous un menu?

I'd like a/an/some...

J'aimerais...

beer	une bière	napkin	une serviette
bread	du pain	oil	de l'huile
butter	du beurre	pepper	du poivre
coffee	un café	potatoes	des pommes
dessert	un dessert		de terre
fish	du poisson	rice	du riz
fork	une fourchette	salad	de la salade
fruit	des fruits	salt	du sel
glass	un verre	sandwich	un sandwich
ice-cream	une glace	soup	de la soupe
knife	un couteau	spoon	une cuiller
meat	de la viande	sugar	du sucre
menu	la carte	tea (mint)	du thé
milk	du lait		(à la menthe)
mineral water	de l'eau miné-	vegetables	des légumes
(fizzy)	rale (gazeuse)	water (iced)	de l'eau (glacée)
mustard	de la moutarde	wine	du vin

...and Read the Menu

abricot	apricot
agneau	lamb
aiglefin	haddock
ail	garlic
ananas	pineapple
artichaut	artichoke
asperge	asparagus
aubergine	aubergine (eggplant)
banane	banana
bar	bass
biftek	beefsteak
bœuf	beef
boulettes	meatballs
brochette	skewered meat
canard	duck
câpres	capers
carottes	carrots
champignons	mushrooms
chou	cabbage
chou-fleur	cauliflower
clémentine	tangerine
concombre	cucumber
confiture	jam
côtelette	chops
courge, courgette	vegetable marrow, zucchini, squash
crème caramel	caramel custard
crevettes	shrimps
dattes	dates
daurade	sea bream
écrevisses	crayfish
épinards	spinach
escargots	snails
faisan	pheasant
figues	figs
flan	custard
flétan	halibut
foie	liver
fraises	strawberries
framboises	raspberries
fromage (de chèvre)	cheese (goat's)
gâteau	cake
ghoraiba	sweet biscuits
haloua	honeyed semolina, halva
homard	lobster
huîtres	oysters
laitue	lettuce
langouste	spiny lobster
maquereau	mackerel
merguez	spicy sausage
morue	codfish
moules	mussels
mulet	grey mullet
navet	turnip
noix	nuts
nouilles	noodles
œufs	eggs
oignons	onions
pamplemousse	grapefruit
pêches	peaches
perche	perch
persil	parsley
poire	pear
pois chiches	chick-peas, garbanzos
pomme	apple
poulet	chicken
raisins	grapes
rognon	kidney
rouget	red mullet
saucisse	sausage
saumon	salmon
tarte	tart, pie
thon	tunafish
tomate	tomato
truite	trout
veau	veal

How to Get There

A reliable travel agent will have full details of all the latest flight possibilities, fares and regulations.

BY AIR

Scheduled flights

Casablanca's airport, Mohamed V, is the principal gateway to Morocco, though both Tangiers and Rabat receive intercontinental traffic, and Agadir and Marrakesh have connections to African and European destinations. The flight from London to Casablanca takes approximately 3 hours, from New York 7 hours.

Charter flights and package tours

From the U.K. and Ireland: Numerous package holidays are available to Morocco, some including flight and hotel or villa, with or without meals. You may take a general tour of the country or a "fixed centre" holiday. You can even choose where you'd like to go and what you'd like to see, then have a package holiday created for you around your specifications.

From North America: Group Inclusive Tours (GIT) are complete package vacations including major sightseeing cities in either Spain or Portugal and Morocco, land arrangements, some meals and the services of an English-speaking guide. Another package tour includes Tangiers on a one-week cruise to the Canary Islands.

BY ROAD AND SEA

From France, the most convenient road leads via Biarritz in the southwest and through Spain via Burgos, Madrid and Málaga to Algeciras, where car ferries operate to Tangiers and Ceuta. There is also a ferry from the French port of Sète to Tangiers, a 36-hour crossing. Be sure you book your ferry passage well in advance, especially in summer.

BY RAIL AND SEA

A direct train links Paris–Irún–Algeciras, where you can cross the Strait of Gibraltar by ferry either to Tangiers or Ceuta. The journey from London to Tangiers takes about 40 hours. Book your ticket a couple of months in advance along with a sleeper or couchette.

The Inter-Rail Card is valid for Morocco, so if you're under 26 you can buy this pass before leaving home. It also entitles the holder to one month's unlimited second-class travel in almost 20 European countries.

When to Go

Although travel agents may say there's no season in Morocco without sun, there are certainly variations in climate worth noting, especially if you plan to see the country inland. In winter there are snowfalls in the high-altitude regions. There can be occasional rain anytime from October to May. In early May the beaches begin to fill with sun-seekers, and from June to September (the dry season) the coast is hot, but humid enough, owing to the softening effects of the sea. Inland, however, the heat can be suffocating in summer.

Temperatures vary greatly between day and night—averages run as much as nine degrees lower at night. The following chart indicates monthly averages for day and sea temperatures:

Tangiers		J	F	M	A	M	J	J	A	S	O	N	D
Air	°C	15	16	17	19	21	24	26	27	25	22	18	16
	°F	59	61	63	66	70	75	79	81	77	72	64	61
Sea	°C	17	17	17	18	20	20	22	23	22	22	20	18
	°F	63	63	63	64	68	68	72	73	72	72	68	64
Agadir		J	F	M	A	M	J	J	A	S	O	N	D
Air	°C	20	21	23	23	24	26	27	27	27	26	24	21
	°F	68	70	73	73	75	79	81	81	81	79	75	70
Sea	°C	17	17	18	18	19	19	22	22	22	22	21	18
	°F	63	63	64	64	66	66	72	72	72	72	70	64

Planning Your Budget

To give you an idea of what to expect, here are some average prices in Moroccan dirhams (DH). They should be considered only as guidelines, as inflation affects prices in Morocco as elsewhere.

Airport transfer. Casablanca airport to town centre: bus 15 DH, taxi 150 DH. Other airports have no public bus service, but taxis are slightly cheaper than at Casablanca.

Baby-sitters. 10 DH per hour.

Bus services. Rabat to Casablanca 40 DH, crosstown trip in one of the main cities 1 DH.

Camping. Adults 5 DH per day, children 3 DH, tent/car/caravan (trailer) 5 DH each.

Car hire (international company). *Renault 4* 130 DH per day, 1.40 DH per km., 1,785 DH per week with unlimited mileage. *Peugeot 205 GR* 165 DH per day, 1.95 DH per km., 2,940 DH per week with unlimited mileage. *Renault 20* 300 DH per day, 2.80 DH per km., 4,900 DH per week with unlimited mileage. Add 12% tax.

Cigarettes (packet of 20). International brands 12 DH, French (dark tobacco) 7.50 DH, Moroccan 1.75–6.80 DH.

Entertainment. Night club (admission and first drink) 75–100 DH, discotheque (admission and first drink) 40 DH, cinema 4.50–7.50 DH.

Guides. 25–30 DH per half-day, 50–60 DH per day.

Hairdressers. *Woman's* cut, shampoo and blow-dry 100 DH, shampoo and blow-dry only, 40–50 DH, permanent wave 120–200 DH. *Man's* cut 35–40 DH.

Hotels (double room with bath or shower and toilet). ***** 350 DH and up (no charge limit), ****A 214 DH, ****B 174 DH, ***A 130 DH, ***B 114 DH, **A 90 DH, **B 74 DH, *A 64 DH, *B 56 DH. Tourist menu 35–65 DH depending on hotel category.

Meals and drinks (in European-style restaurant or bar). Continental breakfast 20 DH, lunch 40–150 DH, dinner 80–300 DH (average price for full meal including drinks in a good restaurant, 150 DH), coffee 2.50 DH, mint tea 2.50 DH, soft drinks 3.25 DH, beer (local, small bottle) 7.50 DH, whisky 20–30 DH.

Taxis. Basic charge 1 DH, 4 DH per km.

Trains (single, first-class ticket). Between Rabat and Meknès 45.50 DH, Marrakesh 61.50 DH, Fez 60.50 DH, Tangiers 76 DH. Second class approx. 35 per cent lower.

BLUEPRINT for a Perfect Trip

An A-Z Summary of Practical Information and Facts

Listed after many entries is the appropriate French translation, usually in the singular, plus a number of phrases to help you when seeking assistance. A star (*) following an entry indicates that relevant prices are to be found on page 103.

AIRPORTS* *(aéroport)*. Morocco's airports are modern, efficient and pleasant places, equipped with most services you might need: restaurant and bar, car hire desks, exchange offices and an information booth.

Duty-free shops are modest and you should not plan to buy much at them. However, in-flight purchases over international waters offer truly astounding savings, even though the selection of goods is limited.

Air transport is possible between El Ayoun, Agadir, Marrakesh, Casablanca, Rabat, Fez, Tangiers, Oujda and Al Hoceima. In some cases it makes more sense to travel by land, as between Casablanca and Rabat, for instance. Domestic services are operated by Royal Air Maroc.

From Casablanca-Mohamed V, the cheapest way to the centre of town is by the airport bus, which takes you to the main bus terminal about every 30 minutes throughout the day; the 20-mile trip takes 45 minutes to one hour by bus. At all other airports you'll have to take a taxi to get into town.

Where's the bus for …?   **Où est l'autobus pour …?**

ALPHABET. See also LANGUAGE. The Arabic alphabet has 28 characters and each of these characters has three different forms, depending on whether it appears at the beginning, in the middle or at the end of a word. Also, the art of calligraphy is highly developed and so the student of Arabic must learn to recognize many styles of writing. It's hardly worth plunging into a study of the language for just a short holiday in Morocco. You can take pleasure from the graceful and intricate inscriptions whether you know the language or not.

Signs and announcements in Morocco are almost always in both French and Arabic, so with a few words of French you should be able to get around quite easily.

BUS SERVICES*. Morocco's largest network of bus routes is operated by C.T.M.-L.N. *(Compagnie de Transports Marocains-Lignes Nationales)*, which has a terminal and garage in every sizable town. Regional buses *(autocar)* tend to have seen much wear and tear, but they still render dependable service. Schedules are kept fairly well. In southern Morocco, S.A.T.A.S. *(Société Anonyme des Transports Automobiles du Souss)* takes up where C.T.M. leaves off. It's advisable to buy your tickets a day or so in advance if possible, and to arrive at the terminal at least a quarter of an hour before the scheduled departure time.

Within Morocco's cities, buses *(autobus)* connect the centre of town with the outskirts and suburbs. As Moroccan cities are mostly small and

B easy to travel around in, the low-priced *petits taxis* (small taxis) are generally preferable to city buses (see TAXIS).

When's the next bus to …?	**Quand part le prochain bus pour … ?**
single (one-way)	**aller simple**
return (round-trip)	**aller et retour**

C **CAMPING*** *(camping).* Morocco is well provided with camping places boasting full facilities for tents and caravans (trailers). Most camp-sites provide showers, electricity and refreshments. The Moroccan National Tourist Office can give you a detailed list of sites. Avoid camping in lonely areas or on unofficial sites (the local police will advise), and be sure to secure your money and valuables.

May we camp here?	**Pouvons-nous camper ici?**
We've a tent/a caravan.	**Nous avons une tente/une caravane.**

CAR HIRE* *(location de voitures).* See also DRIVING IN MOROCCO. The familiar international car-hire firms do business in Morocco, as do many local ones. To be sure of getting exactly the sort of car you want when you want it, reserve in advance through your rental or travel agent at home. Not every vehicle can be driven on unpaved roads *(piste).*

Plan your driving needs carefully, as car hire—once all items are added in—can come out as rather expensive: basic rental, kilometrage, full insurance surcharge, fuel, delivery or return fee and tax add up to a tidy sum. In addition, you will be asked to put down a substantial deposit unless you have a recognized credit card.

I'd like to rent a car (tomorrow).	**Je voudrais louer une voiture (demain).**

CHILDREN*. You will be enchanted by Moroccan children—though you'll have to expect the odd bit of pestering from self-appointed guides, car-watchers, scouts, etc.

Moroccans love children, so if your child wanders off in a *souk,* have no fear; retrace your steps, he'll probably be being looked after by some friendly passer-by or shop-keeper. But if he's really disappeared, of course, you'd best contact the nearest policeman.

The better hotels in Morocco can always arrange for a baby-sitter if given the proper advance notice. The staff will also be able to furnish the necessities for baby care, but you should let them know your needs at the earliest possible moment. The rates on page 103 are for a baby-sitter provided by one of the larger hotels.

Can you get me a baby-sitter for tonight?	**Pouvez-vous me trouver une garde d'enfants pour ce soir?**
I'm looking for my child.	**Je cherche mon enfant.**

CIGARETTES, CIGARS, TOBACCO* (*cigarettes, cigares, tabac*). Major brands of British, American and French cigarettes are readily available at tobacco and newspaper stands *(tabac)* and prices are similar to those in Europe (and slightly higher than in the United States). Local Moroccan products are considerably cheaper than imports.

A variety of cigars are easy to find as well, including the coveted Cuban makes.

Pipe tobacco can be had, but if you're very attached to a particular brand, bring your own supply to avoid disappointment (see ENTRY FORMALITIES AND CUSTOMS CONTROLS).

A packet of .../A box of matches, please.	**Un paquet de .../Une boîte d'allumettes, s'il vous plaît.**
filter-tipped/without filter	**avec/sans filtre**
light/dark tobacco	**du tabac blond/brun**

CLOTHING. To be on the safe side, take a sweater or jacket even in summer as protection against cool night breezes. A raincoat should be part of your gear from mid-November to mid-March. In high summer, cool clothing and a hat against the sun are what's needed.

Though few situations really call for the formality of a jacket and tie or a dress, many people do put on more elegant clothes for dinner in the better hotels.

Don't forget your bathing costume. Even if you are not planning to visit a beach, you'll find some hotels have swimming pools.

COMMUNICATIONS. The main post office *(bureau de postes)* in each city offers full services, including poste restante (general delivery), telegraph and telephone desks.

Hours: 8 a.m. to 6.30 p.m., Monday to Thursday (closed between noon and 2.30 p.m. in smaller towns), and 8 a.m. to noon and 4 to 6.30 p.m. on Fridays.

Main post offices have *permanence* counters which remain open 24 hours a day, every day. (In smaller towns such as Agadir, the "permanence" may only extend to 9 p.m.) These special departments provide

C telephone and telegraph services and stamp sales. Stamps can also be purchased at tobacconists'.

Poste restante (general delivery): On a short trip, it's often impractical to await mail, as delays are frequent and unpredictable. Both outgoing and incoming post may be held up, so a cable or telephone call is more reliable in case of necessity. For longer stays, have mail sent to your hotel, or to poste restante, addressed this way:

> Name
> Poste Restante
> City, Morocco

Go to the central or principal post office to pick up poste-restante mail. Hours vary somewhat (see above). Take your passport and be prepared to pay a small fee for each letter received.

Telephone: Should you have to place an international call, it may go through in minutes or it may take the better part of a day. Though most of your dealing with the telephone will be routine and relatively problem-free, it's good to keep this in mind.

Telephone service throughout Morocco is automatic. If you are a subscriber, direct-dialling to much of Europe is also possible, but unless you are reversing the charges you will have to let your hotel switchboard or the post office switchboard make arrangements for the call and for payment.

Public pay telephones can be found in cafés and public places such as railway and bus stations. Cashiers can provide you with the proper coins.

> Dial: 10 for operator
> 16 for information
> 14 for telegrams
> 12 for international calls

Can you get me this number in …?	**Pouvez-vous me donner ce numéro à …?**
Have you received any mail for …?	**Avez-vous du courrier pour …?**
A stamp for this letter/postcard, please.	**Un timbre pour cette lettre/carte postale, s'il vous plaît.**
express (general delivery)	**exprès**
airmail	**par avion**
registered	**recommandé**
I want to send a telegram to …	**J'aimerais envoyer un télégramme à …**

COMPLAINTS. Moroccans are usually very accommodating when it comes to ironing out misunderstandings over service or prices, but if you run into trouble, your first recourse should be to higher authority in the establishment concerned. If the manager can't be found, or is of no help, a policeman can often act as an informal and disinterested arbiter to straighten things out.

A rule which helps to avoid many misunderstandings is always to settle on a price in advance, whether it be for a carriage ride, a carpet or a guide in the markets. (Licensed guides operate according to a fixed schedule of charges, which they must not exceed. As for unofficial guides, they are everywhere and will provide their services whether asked to or not.)

Guides, hotels and restaurants are required by law to have complaints books *(livre de réclamations)* ready to hand at all times. If you are displeased with services or prices, you can register your complaint in the book and it should be dealt with by the government inspectors who check the books periodically.

CONSULATES and EMBASSIES

Canada (embassy and consulate): 13 bis, Rue Jaafar As-Sadik, Rabat (Agdal); tel. 713-75.

United Kingdom (embassy and consulate): 17, Boulevard de la Tour Hassan, Rabat; tel. 209-05.

Consulate General: 60, Boulevard d'Anfa, Casablanca; tel. 22-17-41/ 22-16-53/22-31-85.

Tangiers Office of the British Embassy in Rabat: 9, Rue Amérique du Sud, Tangiers; tel. 358-95/96/97.

U.S.A. (embassy and consulate): 2, Avenue de Marrakech, Rabat; tel. 622-65.

Consulate General: 9, Boulevard Moulay Youssef, Casablanca; tel. 26-05-21.

Consulate General: Chemin des Amoureux, Tangiers; tel. 394-81/ 353-17.

CONVERTER CHARTS. For fluid and distance measures, see page 111. Morocco uses the metric system.

C Temperature

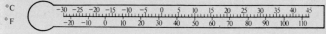

Length

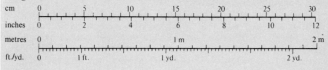

Weight

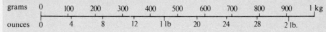

D DRIVING IN MOROCCO

Entering Morocco: You will need:

- a valid driving licence (national or international)
- car registration papers
- a Green Card (an extension of your car insurance policy to cover travel in Morocco; if you have no Green Card, you'll be required to purchase Moroccan insurance at the border)
- a *carnet* is needed for a caravan (trailer); see your home automobile association. You may encounter difficulties in entering Morocco at Ceuta or Tangiers; inquire at the Moroccan embassy before departure.

Driving Conditions: Regulations are virtually identical with French ones and are similar in most respects to those of Europe in general. Morocco has perhaps the best-maintained and most extensive road system in North Africa and, while not subject to extremely heavy traffic, many roads are certainly well used. The final stretch of the motorway (superhighway) connecting Casablanca with Rabat is under construction, but it will take some years before work is completed.

The country also has miles of unsurfaced routes and mountain and desert tracks called *pistes.* Such roads in mountain areas are often impassable during the rainy season, from November to the end of April, with a slight let-up in January to February. Fords tend at this season to be under water, as they do when the snows melt. Beware, too, of

110

snowfalls that occur between December and May in the mountain regions.

Remember that many country people are not good at judging the speed of oncoming cars and if someone is crossing the road or about to cross, slow down to avoid an accident. As virtually all roads are two-lane only, heavy vehicles and motorcycles must be passed with caution. It is best to avoid driving at night because of pedestrians, animals and vehicles without lights in the roadway.

Your headlights must be modified to dip to the right; automobile clubs and accessories shops sell devices for this purpose.

Drive on the right.

Traffic Police: Officers of the Sûreté Nationale patrol major highways to watch for violations and to aid motorists in distress. You are certain to encounter at least one checkpoint in your travels, at which motorcycle policemen will ask to see your car registration documents, insurance certificate and driving licence. The check—if all is in order—is a matter of a minute or so.

Fuel and oil: As petrol stations are usually concentrated in major cities and towns, it's a good practice to fill up your tank as you leave a city for the open road.

Fluid measures

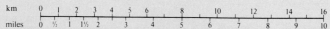

Distances: Here are some approximate road distances in kilometres between major centres:

Rabat–Casablanca	90	Marrakesh–Goulimine	465
Rabat–Tangiers	280	Casablanca–Agadir	490
Rabat–Marrakesh	325	Fez–Meknès	60
Marrakesh–Ouarzazate	205	Meknès–Tangiers	270
Marrakesh–Agadir	255	Fez–Marrakesh	485

To convert kilometres to miles:

Breakdowns: Major cities have good garages and knowledge of French cars is common. Other European makes usually present no great problem and most of the time parts can be had fairly easily. Some

British vehicles (especially the ubiquitous Land Rover) are well known and easily serviced.

Parking: A *gardien* will expect a tip after he has helped you to park or unpark your car. But his willingness to help is no guarantee that your car is parked legally and if you don't obey the signs, it may be towed away.

Road signs: Directional signs are in both French and Arabic. Most road signs are of the common European pictograph variety. Some of the more common written ones (bilingual) are these:

Arrêt	Stop
Attention	Caution
Attention travaux	Caution: road works
Cédez	Yield; give way
Crue	Liable to flood during rains
Défense de stationner	No parking
Déviation	Diversion (detour)
Lentement	Slow
Serrez à droite	Keep to the right
Virages	Bends (curves)

(international) driving licence	**permis de conduire (international)**
car registration papers	**permis de circulation**
insurance card	**certificat d'assurance**
Are we on the right road to …?	**Sommes-nous sur la route de …?**
Fill the tank, please.	**Faites le plein, s'il vous plaît.**
normal/super	**normale/super**
Check the oil/tires/battery.	**Veuillez contrôler l'huile/les pneus/la batterie.**
I've had a breakdown.	**Ma voiture est en panne.**
There's been an accident	**Il y a eu un accident.**

DRUGS. Morocco was once the land of hashish and *kif,* and you may still come upon an old man or two sitting at a village tea house enjoying a minuscule pipeful of the drug, but police are on the lookout for users of drugs as a whole, and penalties can be stiff.

ELECTRIC CURRENT. Voltages of 110 and 220 exist side by side in Morocco and you should always check which you have before plugging in. Most times the voltage will be indicated on the socket. Outlets and plugs are of the French type. Power surges are a bothersome occurrence and so it's best not to leave any appliance connected when not in use: unplug your razor or a surge may damage the transformer.

What's the voltage—110 or 220?	**Quel est le voltage – cent dix (110) ou deux cent vingt (220)?**
a battery	**une pile**

EMERGENCIES. Depending on the nature of the problem, refer to the separate entries in this section such as CONSULATES, MEDICAL CARE, POLICE, etc.

Hotel staff are ready to help in emergencies, as are officers of the Sûreté Nationale and local police. Special telephone numbers for fire or ambulance (dial 15) and police (dial 19) are available in the major cities.

ENTRY FORMALITIES and CUSTOMS CONTROLS *(douane)*. See also DRIVING IN MOROCCO. For most tourists, including citizens of the U.K., U.S.A., Eire, Canada, Australia and New Zealand, only a valid passport is necessary to enter Morocco.

The British Embassy advises travellers intending to remain in Morocco for periods longer than three weeks to register at the nearest British Representation at Rabat, Casablanca or Tangiers.

The following chart shows what main duty-free items you may take into Morocco and, when returning home, into your own country.

Into:	Cigarettes		Cigars		Tobacco	Spirits	Wine
Morocco	200	or 50	or	250 g.		1 and 1	
Australia	200	or 250 g.	or	250 g.		1 l. or	1 l.
Canada	200	and 50	and	900 g.		1.1 l. or	1.1 l.
Eire	200	or 50	or	250 g.		1 l. and	2 l.
N.Zealand	200	or 50	or	250 g.		1.1 l. and	4.5 l.
U.K.	200	or 50	or	250 g.		1 l. and	2 l.
U.S.A.	200	and 100	and	*		1 l. or	1 l.

*a reasonable quantity

E **Currency restrictions:** Import and export of dirhams is not permitted. You can bring as much foreign currency into or out of Morocco as you like (though amounts in excess of the equivalent of 5,000 dirhams must be declared on entry to enable you to reexport the same sum). You can take out up to 50 per cent of the total amount exchanged on arrival if your stay is longer than 48 hours. For a short stay of under 48 hours, you can take out up to 100 per cent of the currency you exchanged. To be on the safe side, don't change your money all at once, but according to your needs of the moment.

Save your currency exchange receipts: it's a simple matter to change small amounts of dirhams into another currency at the border or airport as you leave.

I've nothing to declare.	**Je n'ai rien à déclarer.**
It's for my personal use.	**C'est pour mon usage personnel.**

G **GUIDES and INTERPRETERS*** *(guide; interprète).* All official guides must be approved and licensed by the Moroccan National Tourist Office and must carry official identification cards with them. The local branch of the Tourist Office or *Syndicat d'initiative* can arrange for a licensed guide; often several will be waiting at the office to be hired. The greatest number speak French; next most common language is English. For other languages, make reservations in advance.

We'd like an English-speaking guide.	**Nous aimerions un guide parlant anglais.**
Do you have a licence?	**Est-ce que vous êtes agréé?**
I need an English interpreter.	**J'ai besoin d'un interprète anglais.**

H **HAGGLING.** Some of the fancier shops have fixed prices and will tell you so. In the *médina* you may see price tags on goods, but the chances are the shopkeeper will be open to bargaining. Visit a few shops to compare prices before you begin serious haggling, and if you are energetic (without being discourteous), you will end up paying considerably less than the initially quoted price. Even if you dislike haggling, you should never accept a starting price, as it's accepted practice in Morocco to bargain.

HAIRDRESSERS"* *(coiffeur).* Facilities range from the sybaritic salons of the grand hotels to a folding chair under a plastic tarpaulin in the *médina.* Unless you want a very close crop at a very low price, stay with the larger hotels.

Tipping: what you pay for your haircut or shampoo goes into the coffers of the shop and so you should tip the person who actually worked with you. The normal tip is 10–15 per cent of the charge.

H

HITCH-HIKING *(auto-stop).* You'll pass more Moroccan hitch-hikers than foreign ones and if you have room, a local person will be very appreciative of a ride. Foreigners often find bus travel in Morocco so cheap that they take the bus in preference.

Can you give me a lift to …? **Pouvez-vous m'emmener à …?**

HOTELS and ACCOMMODATION* *(hôtel; logement).* See also CAMPING and YOUTH HOSTELS. Hotels are rated by the government and prices are controlled, except for the top-class establishments.

The highest rating is five stars. One- to four-star hotels are subdivided into "A" and "B" categories. Those in the three-, four- or five-star categories are very often booked solid in spring, summer and autumn and reservations should be made in advance. Even with reservations (taken lightly by some hotel managements) you should plan to arrive fairly early in the day to claim your room. Be sure to carry official confirmation. Simpler hotels rating one and two stars have less of a crowding problem, but it is still advisable to arrive in good time to find a room. Though Morocco is doing much to remedy its shortage of hotel rooms, demand will outstrip supply for some time yet.

The rates on page 103 (single rooms are approximately 35 per cent less) do not include meals, though in high season the management may try to persuade you to purchase full-board arrangements. For convenience's sake you may elect to take your meals in the hotel and you should be aware that prices for the standard tourist breakfast and *menu touristique* are also set by the government and depend on the class of hotel. All these prices must be posted conspicuously in your room.

a single/double room **une chambre à un lit/deux lits**
What's the rate per night? **Quel est le prix pour une nuit?**

HOURS. See also MONEY MATTERS and COMMUNICATIONS. Museum and monument visiting hours tend to be erratic and extremely subject to change, so it's more than advisable to check with each city's tourist office before venturing there. Here, however, is a round-up of those mentioned in the book:

H **Fez**

Borj Nord: 8.30 a.m.–noon and 2.30–6 p.m. (4–6 p.m. on Fridays) daily except Tuesday.

Marrakesh

Bahia Palace, Dar Si Saïd and Tombs of the Saadians: 8.30 a.m.–12.30 p.m. and 2.30–6.30 p.m. daily except Tuesday.

Meknès

Koubbet el Khiyatîn and Bou Inania médersa: 9 a.m.–noon and 3–6.30 p.m. daily.

Moulay Ismaïl's tomb: no definite hours.

Rabat

Mausoleum of Mohammed V: 8 a.m.–9 p.m. daily.

Musée des Oudaïa: 8.30 a.m.–noon and 4–6.30 p.m. daily except Tuesday.

Archaeological Museum: 8.30 a.m.–noon and 2–7 p.m. (2–6 p.m. in winter) daily except Tuesday.

Tangiers

Dar el Makhzen, Museum of Moroccan Arts and Antiquities Museum: 8.30 a.m.–12.15 p.m. and 2.30–5.45 p.m., closed on Sundays and public holidays.

L **LANGUAGE.** See also ALPHABET and box on page 20. Although the official language of Morocco is Arabic, French is very widely understood and spoken: in big towns, just about everybody has a smattering, however small. In the north around Tangiers and Tétouan (formerly under Spanish control), Spanish is more frequently known than French. Staff concerned with airlines and major hotels may know English and perhaps another European language such as Italian or German, but you shouldn't depend completely on English being understood.

Even though French is so widely spoken, you may come into contact with people in the countryside who know no French, only Arabic or Berber, so that mastery of a few basic Arabic expressions is greatly appreciated:

Good morning	**S'báh 'l khéyr**
Good afternoon	**Msá 'l khéyr**
116 Good night	**Tas'báh alláh**

Please	**Min fádlak, áfak**
Thank you	**Bárakallahúfik, shókran**
You're welcome	**Mrába**
Goodbye	**Beslémeh**

The Berlitz phrase books FRENCH FOR TRAVELLERS and ARABIC FOR TRAVELLERS will help in most situations you're likely to encounter in Morocco. In addition, the Berlitz French-English/English-French pocket dictionary contains 12,500 concepts.

LAUNDRY and DRY-CLEANING *(blanchissage; nettoyage à sec).* Your hotel can arrange to have laundry and dry-cleaning done, even if you are staying in a modest, one-star establishment. For laundry you may reasonably expect 24-hour service, but dry-cleaning may take two to four days. You may save a dirham or two by seeking out a dry-cleaning shop on your own.

| When will it be ready? | **Quand est-ce que ce sera prêt?** |
| I must have this for tomorrow morning. | **Il me le faut pour demain matin.** |

LOST PROPERTY. Hotel, restaurant and café personnel can generally be relied on to keep your forgotten book, hat or purse safe at the *caisse* (cash desk). Make the rounds of places you've visited as soon as you discover the loss. On buses and trains, ask any official; there's always an established mechanism for tracing lost goods.

| I've lost my wallet/handbag/passport. | **J'ai perdu mon portefeuille/sac à main/passeport.** |

MAPS. The Moroccan National Tourist Office hands out free brochures containing general, undetailed maps of the country. Several good road maps of the country are available at news-stands and bookshops. Here, you will also find city street plans and more expensive handy maps with street indexes to Casablanca, Rabat and Marrakesh.

The maps in this book were prepared by Falk-Verlag, Hamburg.

| a street plan of... | **un plan de...** |
| a road map of this region | **une carte routière de cette région** |

M **MEDICAL CARE.** See also EMERGENCIES. If your home health insurance doesn't cover you abroad, you may wish to take out insurance which does, or talk to your agent about extending your coverage. In the U.K., check with your local Social Security office well in advance of your departure.

Moroccan cities all have at least one hospital and as doctors from abroad also work in the country, you may even be able to find one who speaks English. Embassies, consulates and large hotels will know which hospitals, clinics and doctors to recommend.

Chemists' shops, or pharmacies *(pharmacie),* are conveniently located in all cities and most towns and are open during normal business hours. Outside these hours, ask at your hotel for the name and location of the *pharmacie de service* or *pharmacie de nuit.* Bring a supply of your medicine if you take any regularly, for local pharmacies may not be able to fill a foreign prescription exactly.

Standards of hygiene are quite adequate in the better hotels and restaurants in Morocco, and bottled water is easily to be had. The most common tourist malaise is caused by too much sun, strange food, walking. The rule for good health is everything in moderation.

A malaria risk exists between May and October in some country districts, but urban areas are quite safe. Inoculations against polio, typhoid and tetanus and injections of gamma globulin against hepatitis are recommended. To be on the safe side, drink bottled water.

Where's the chemist on duty?	**Où est la pharmacie de service?**
I need a doctor.	**Il me faut un médecin.**
I've a pain here.	**J'ai mal ici.**
a fever	**de la fièvre**
an upset stomach	**mal à l'estomac**
sunburn	**un coup de soleil**

MEETING PEOPLE. Morocco is actually two societies in one. Educated, modern Moroccans are often bilingual French-Arabic and are totally familiar with European social customs. Traditional Moroccans, out in the countryside, speaking only Arabic or Berber, follow the strict and timeless Islamic code.

Moroccans are immensely hospitable by nature, and appreciate easy and open contacts with visitors. They do not expect you to know Arabic and greet you in French (or Spanish), whether they speak that language fluently or not. Should you venture an Arabic greeting, the response **118** will be positively enthusiastic (see LANGUAGE).

It's customary to shake hands at each encounter. The tradition-minded will then place his right hand (the one you shake with) briefly on his heart.

MONEY MATTERS

Currency: Morocco's unit of currency is the *dirham,* abbreviated *DH,* which is divided into 100 *centimes.*

Coins: 5, 10, 20, 50 centimes and 1 dirham.

Banknotes: 5, 10, 50, 100 dirhams.

Moroccan merchants will often use the word *francs* when they mean centimes.

For currency restrictions, see under ENTRY FORMALITIES AND CUSTOMS CONTROLS.

Banking hours: In general banks *(banque)* are open:
Summer: 8.15–11.30 a.m. and 2.15–4 p.m., Monday to Thursday, 8.15–11.30 a.m. and 3.15–5 p.m. on Fridays.
Winter: 8.30–11.30 a.m. and 2.30–4.30 p.m., Monday to Friday.

Major hotels and travel agencies are also authorized to change foreign currency. If you're really in trouble, try the exchange bureau *(bureau de change)* at the nearest airport, which will be open as long as international flights are departing or arriving, no matter what day it is.

During the holy month of Ramadan, special hours of operation apply to all businesses.

Credit Cards and Traveller's Cheques: Traveller's cheques *(chèque de voyage)* are readily recognized and accepted at banks. Some shops and airlines will take them as well. Credit cards *(carte de crédit)* can be used in the large hotels and some of the best restaurants, but it's always advisable to ask in advance whether your card or cheques will be accepted. Eurocheques are accepted by some banks and many tourist-oriented establishments in the main cities.

Be sure to have your passport with you whenever you intend to use your credit card, exchange notes or pay with a traveller's cheque. Keep the exchange slips just in case you have left-over dirhams which you want to change back when you leave the country.

I would like to change some pounds/dollars.	**J'aimerais changer des livres sterling/des dollars.**
Do you accept traveller's cheques?	**Acceptez-vous les chèques de voyage?**
Can I pay with this credit card?	**Puis-je payer avec cette carte de crédit?**

M MOTORCYCLE HIRE *(location de motocyclettes)*. In Marrakesh and Tangiers you can hire a motorcycle, small or large, by the hour, the day or the week. Rental charges are about the same as for a small car. You must be in possession of a valid driving licence. Bicycles are not yet a popular rental item in Morocco.

N NEWSPAPERS and MAGAZINES *(journal; revue)*. In the major cities, hotel news-stands, newspaper kiosks and some bookstores stock certain British, American and European newspapers. A few of the most popular English-language magazines are sold as well. Newspapers may be a day or two late and for one reason or another may be unavailable from time to time.

Have you any English-language newspapers/magazines?	**Avez-vous des journaux/revues de langue anglaise?**

P PETS. Morocco allows cats and dogs in if they are accompanied by a veterinarian good-health certificate from your home country. The problems begin on your return journey. U.S. and Canadian authorities demand a certificate of rabies vaccination for your pet and reserve the right to impose quarantine. The British and Irish automatically quarantine any animal for six full months—with no possibility of appeal whatsoever.

PHOTOGRAPHY. Well-stocked photography shops (which also make minor repairs) exist in the large cities. Although they can handle both black-and-white and colour developing (in Agadir many shops advertise 24-hour colour developing service, faster than in other cities), you may avoid occasional delay and disappointment by waiting until your return to have film developed. If you purchase film (the price is prohibitive), be sure to check the expiry date and be sure it hasn't been stored in the heat or sunlight.

I'd like a film for this camera.	**J'aimerais un film pour cet appareil.**
a black-and-white film	**un film noir et blanc**
a film for colour prints	**un film couleurs**
a colour-slide film	**un film pour diapositives**
How long will it take to develop (and print) this film?	**Combien de temps faut-il pour développer (et tirer) ce film?**
Can I take a picture?	**Puis-je prendre une photo?**

POLICE. Local police *(police)* work closely with the national police force *(Sûreté Nationale)*. Moroccan policemen are courteous and very willing to help. In some of the major cities you can dial 19 to reach the special emergency police force.

Morocco is traditional in many ways, one of the more delightful being the low incidence of crime and thefts. Still, no country is without pickpockets (be on guard in the *médinas*) or those who will break a car window if they see a camera or handbag on the seat. Normal precautions will suffice. Have your hotel receptionist keep any valuables in the safe.

Where's the nearest police station?	**Où se trouve le poste de police le plus proche?**
I want to report a theft.	**Je veux signaler un vol.**
My ... has been stolen.	**On a volé mon...**
wallet/handbag/ passport	**portefeuille/sac à main/ passeport**

PUBLIC HOLIDAYS *(jour férié)*. The major religious festivals are dated according to the Islamic lunar calendar, which means that the holy days occur about eleven days earlier each year, according to our system. The year begins with the month of Moharrem; *Moharrem 1st* (the Moslem New Year's Day) is a public holiday. On the 10th day of Moharrem, *Achoura*, a New Year's festival is celebrated with special traditional foods and activities. The next major feast day comes at *Mouloud*, or the birthday of the Prophet, when merry-making extends over two days and shops are closed. During *Ramadan*, everyone is supposed to fast between sunrise and sunset, but once the sun goes down, one can eat as much as one wants. Special business hours come into effect during Ramadan and virtually nothing is allowed to stand in the way of a hungry Moslem on his way home to his first meal since early morning. (Some restaurants and cafés stay open to serve non-Moslems.) To celebrate the end of Ramadan, *Id el-Fitr*, or *Id es-Seghir*, "the lesser festival" is a two-day period of rejoicing and lots of food. The *Id el-Adha*, or *Id el-Kebir*, "the greater festival", commemorates the near-sacrifice by Abraham of his son. Festivities last two days and all shops and businesses are closed.

For the dates of these important holidays, ask at any tourist office or hotel desk.

Other principal holidays are the *Fête du Trône* (Accession of King Hassan II) on March 3, the *Fête de la Jeunesse* (Youth Festival) on **121**

P July 9 and on November 18 celebrating the triumphal return of Mohammed V from exile to full rule.

Are you open tomorrow? **Etes-vous ouvert demain?**

R **RADIO and TV** *(radio; télévision).* Moroccan radio and television stations broadcast in both Arabic and French. Because Morocco is so close to Spain and to Gibraltar, one can often tune in to Spanish- and English-language radio programmes and in Tangiers, to Spanish television programmes as well. With moderately good reception conditions all the strongest radio stations of Europe can also be received.

RELIGIOUS SERVICES. The religion of Morocco is Islam, but French and Spanish influence has left at least one Roman Catholic church in each city and large town. Protestant churches are found in Agadir, Casablanca, Rabat, Fez, Marrakesh and Meknès, as are synagogues. In Casablanca it's possible to attend Orthodox services, the majority of which are in French. Ask at your hotel reception desk for the address of the desired church or synagogue.

S **SIESTA.** The gracious custom of afternoon siesta, so sensible in countries with a hot summer climate, is rigidly observed in Morocco, and the country virtually closes down between the hours of 12 noon and 3.30 p.m. on weekdays. Cafés are the most prominent exception, but otherwise the list of closings includes banks, shops and offices.

T **TAXI*.** Taxis in Morocco are of two types: small cars painted blue or red with a rooftop luggage rack and the legend *Petit Taxi* (little taxi) and larger cars, often American makes, sometimes bright blue. *Petits taxis* are inexpensive and most have meters. These small cars are not supposed to take tourists on long trips outside the city limits. The larger cars *(grand taxi)* are slightly more expensive, and no limit is set on where they can go. Within city limits, rates for these cabs go according to the meter. For tours in the country, strike a bargain with the driver before starting the ride.

All taxis charge 50 per cent extra between the hours of 8 p.m. and 6 a.m.

122

It's customary to give a small tip to the driver. Rounding off the fare is sufficient most of the time.

What's the fare to...?   **Quel est le tarif pour...?**

TIME DIFFERENCES. Morocco time is GMT, but some years the clocks are put forward in summer. The following chart shows the time in January in some selected cities.

New York	London	**Morocco**	Sydney	Auckland
7 a.m.	noon	**noon**	11 p.m.	1 a.m.

What time is it, please?   **Quelle heure est-il, s'il vous plaît?**

TOILETS *(toilettes).* If your hotel room has a toilet it will be kept in good condition. Public toilets, rare except in large hotels, airports and open-air cafés, may leave something to be desired. By buying a cup of coffee or a mint tea you gain the right to use a café's facilities. Though toilets adjacent to hotel lobbies are meant for guests and visitors, no one will quibble if it's an emergency. In some toilets you may have to tip the attendant a few centimes.

Dames indicates Ladies, and *Messieurs,* Gentlemen.

Where are the toilets?   **Où sont les toilettes?**

TOURIST INFORMATION OFFICES *(office de tourisme).* The Moroccan National Tourist Office *(Office National Marocain du Tourisme—O. N. M. T.)* maintains branches in major tourist centres in Morocco and in several foreign countries.

Offices abroad of the O. N. M. T.:

Canada: 2, Carlton Street, Suite 1803, Toronto, Ont. M5B 1K2; tel.: (416) 598-2208/10.

United Kingdom: 174, Regent Street, London W1R 6HB; tel.: (01) 437-0013 and 437-0074.

T **U.S.A.:** 20 East 46th Street, Suite 503, New York, NY 10017; tel.: (212) 557-2520-22.

EPCOT Center (Walt Disney World), FL 32830; tel.: (305) 827-5337.

In Morocco, tourist offices are located in all major towns.

Where's the tourist office? **Où se trouve le Syndicat d'initiative?**

TRAINS* *(train)*. The Office National des Chemins de Fer du Maroc (O.N.C.F.M.) operates trains between Tangiers and Marrakesh via Rabat and Casablanca; Tangiers and Oujda via Meknès and Fez; and between Casablanca and Oujda. High-speed trains operate between Rabat and Casablanca and Casablanca and Marrakesh. Certain trains offer three classes of travel. Although full meals are not available, you can usually obtain sandwiches and soft drinks. Some trains provide sleeping accommodation in the form either of couchettes or sleeping cars *(wagons-lits)* which are air-conditioned. Reserve sleeping accommodation well in advance to avoid disappointment. Punctuality is not all that common, but you should be at the station a few minutes early just in case. Yes, trains have been known to leave before the scheduled departure time.

Morocco is included in the territory covered by the Inter-Rail Card.

W **WATER** *(eau)*. Water from the tap is usually safe to drink in Morocco, and in fact that is exactly what you will be served (free of charge) in more modest restaurants. However, bottled mineral water is often kinder to sensitive stomachs and certainly tastier and more healthful. It is always available in restaurants, cafés and hotels. *Sidi Harazem* and *Sidi Ali* (still) and *Oulmès* (fizzy) are the country's most popular springs.

a bottle of mineral water
 carbonated/non-carbonated

une bouteille d'eau minérale gazeuse/non-gazeuse

Is this drinking water? **Est-ce de l'eau potable?**

Y **YOUTH HOSTELS** *(auberge de jeunesse)*. These establishments tend to be very basic, even for youth hostels. Rates are rock-bottom, but you may find a one-star hotel has slightly better and more suitable facilities for only a dirham or two more.

SOME USEFUL EXPRESSIONS

yes/no	**oui/non**
please/thank you	**s'il vous plaît/merci**
excuse me	**excusez-moi**
you're welcome	**je vous en prie**
where/when/how	**où/quand/comment**
how long/how far	**combien de temps/à quelle distance**
yesterday/today/tomorrow	**hier/aujourd'hui/demain**
day/week/month/year	**jour/semaine/mois/année**
left/right	**gauche/droite**
up/down	**en haut/en bas**
good/bad	**bon/mauvais**
big/small	**grand/petit**
cheap/expensive	**bon marché/cher**
hot/cold	**chaud/froid**
old/new	**vieux/neuf**
open/closed	**ouvert/fermé**
here/there	**ici/là**
free (vacant)/occupied	**libre/occupé**
early/late	**tôt/tard**
easy/difficult	**facile/difficile**

Does anyone here speak English?	**Y a-t-il quelqu'un ici qui parle anglais?**
What does this mean?	**Que signifie ceci?**
I don't understand.	**Je ne comprends pas.**
Please write it down.	**Veuillez bien me l'écrire.**
Is there an admission charge?	**Y a-t-il des frais d'entrée?**
Waiter!	**Garçon!**
I'd like…	**J'aimerais…**
How much is that?	**C'est combien?**
Have you something less expensive?	**Avez-vous quelque chose de moins cher?**
What time is it?	**Quelle heure est-il?**
Help me please.	**Aidez-moi, s'il vous plaît.**
Get a doctor—quickly!	**Un médecin, vite!**

125

DAYS OF THE WEEK

Sunday	**dimanche**	Thursday	**jeudi**
Monday	**lundi**	Friday	**vendredi**
Tuesday	**mardi**	Saturday	**samedi**
Wednesday	**mercredi**		

MONTHS

January	**janvier**	July	**juillet**
February	**février**	August	**août**
March	**mars**	September	**septembre**
April	**avril**	October	**octobre**
May	**mai**	November	**novembre**
June	**juin**	December	**décembre**

NUMBERS

0	**zéro**	19	**dix-neuf**
1	**un, une**	20	**vingt**
2	**deux**	21	**vingt et un**
3	**trois**	22	**vingt-deux**
4	**quatre**	23	**vingt-trois**
5	**cinq**	30	**trente**
6	**six**	40	**quarante**
7	**sept**	50	**cinquante**
8	**huit**	60	**soixante**
9	**neuf**	70	**soixante-dix**
10	**dix**	71	**soixante et onze**
11	**onze**	80	**quatre-vingts**
12	**douze**	90	**quatre-vingt-dix**
13	**treize**	100	**cent**
14	**quatorze**	101	**cent un**
15	**quinze**	126	**cent vingt-six**
16	**seize**	200	**deux cents**
17	**dix-sept**	300	**trois cents**
18	**dix-huit**	1000	**mille**

Index

An asterisk (*) next to a page number indicates a map reference. The French names given in brackets behind certain entries correspond to the designations found on the maps.